# Christian Soldier

*How do you act like a Christian while holding a gun to someone's face?*

Ben Adams

authorHOUSE®

*AuthorHouse™*
*1663 Liberty Drive, Suite 200*
*Bloomington, IN 47403*
*www.authorhouse.com*
*Phone: 1-800-839-8640*

*First published by AuthorHouse 11/12/2008*

*ISBN: 978-1-4389-0524-2 (sc)*
*ISBN: 978-1-4389-0525-9 (hc)*

*Library of Congress Control Number: 2008907911*

*Printed in the United States of America*
*Bloomington, Indiana*

*This book is printed on acid-free paper.*

*Edited by Sarah Jo R. Lorenz*

*For Lavonne, Ben and Gladys*

# Table of Contents

Forward                                   ix
Because Life                              1
The Clown Lamp                            7
Beat It!                                  15
To Tame a Land                            24
Gain                                      37
Marine                                    42
Loss                                      53
Friends                                   56
See you in a year                         67
Me and Jesus                              82
What He Didn't Say…                       86
Learn                                     101
The Black Spidey Suit                     103
Inappropriate                             110
Because God                               113
A Moment                                  125
Special Thanks…                           131
Soundtrack                                133

# Forward

*In the Summer of 2007,* the blockbuster movie Spiderman 3 came to the big screen. At thousands of movie theaters across the country, the poster for this movie depicted two Spidermans looking at each other in the glass of a high-rise skyscraper. One Spiderman wore the traditional red and blue Spidey suit. The other Spiderman wore the Black Spidey suit. In addition, one could read the words "The Battle Within" next to the two web-slingers. This movie poster captured the internal struggle of all human beings throughout time. That is, controlling one's thoughts and behaviors in a positive, God-focused manner, or having one's thoughts and behaviors tilt away from God, in a more self-focused, negative manner.

Whether people acknowledge it or not, there is a titanic battle raging between these two polar-opposite positions. This battle is raging not only in every person in the United States, but in every person, in every country around the world. In this book, Ben Adams not only captures this internal battle within us, he describes it in raw, vivid, and emotional detail.

He shows us this struggle within the individuals he has encountered in his life. You will see it in the domestic violence Ben and his family endured during his childhood and adolescence. You will see and feel the physical aggression Ben and his brother encounter growing up in South Florida. You will experience it within the individuals Ben comes across as a soldier, deputy sheriff, and as a deacon in his church.

He also shows us this constant battle within himself as a boy growing up in Texas and Florida, as well as a young man in boot camp on Parris Island, South Carolina and during his tour of duty in Iraq.

In Christian Soldier, you get the insight and privilege of hearing Ben's thoughts and emotions, as well as the behaviors that follow in this massive, internal Donnie-brook. Indeed, as Ben states "I'm not the first to recognize an internal struggle within our souls. You see, recognizing it isn't the problem for me. The problem is the addiction to both."

Most importantly, Ben shows all of us how to win this battle to glorify God's name. He accomplishes this through helping us understand how important a relationship with Jesus Christ is, and specifically through a beautifully laid-out description of how this relationship changes us from the inside out. He also helps us win the battle through Scripture. He places Scripture at opportune times in order to address the issues, struggles, thoughts, and emotions we will most likely have over the course of our lives. Finally, he helps us win the internal struggle, and glorify God's name through his own life story. Ben draws on many stories within his difficult childhood, challenging adolescence, and character-producing young adulthood to show you how he thought and felt, emotionally, in developing his position that he will serve and glorify God's name. Indeed, Ben is known to quote the Scripture "As for me and my family, we will serve the Lord" Joshua 24:15.

During the reading of this book, I experienced many emotions and at the same time learned how to better glorify God's name. I was sad, angry, and in tears while reading about Ben's experiences as a child, as well as his experiences as a deputy sheriff. I welcomed those emotions. I felt happiness, joy, excitement, (and shed more tears) as I read about his relationship with Jesus Christ. I especially welcomed those emotions. It is hoped that you, too, will have a unique, emotional, and learning experience on the way to glorifying God's name on a daily basis.

David L. Modders, Ph.D.
Ocala, Florida
June 21st, 2008

# Because Life

*It was about 6:30 in* the morning and I was driving rental SUV down a lightly traveled road well known for prostitution. I was wearing a light-blue dress shirt, beige trousers that were cuffed and pleated, and brown slip on shoes with tassels. I had a nervous albeit excited feeling in the pit of my stomach. It almost felt as if I were doing something horribly wrong. Then I saw her. She was around 40 years old, wearing a dirty white t-shirt, dirty blue jeans and was smoking a cigarette with another girl. I pulled up while rolling down my window and asked, "You wanna make some money?"

She looked at me, smiled and told me she wasn't just going to hop in. She told me she thought I was the police.

I replied, "do you wanna make some money or not?"

She was still hesitant.

I pulled over and stepped out.

She grabbed for my crotch and asked if I was "the police." I told her no and asked her if she was. The other young lady standing with her reached over and grabbed my crotch and confirmed, "he ain't the police," with a smile. The older lady walked around the rental car and got in the passenger seat and said "let's go."

I was picking up a prostitute. The deal was going to be, I would pay her $40 …and she would give me oral sex. Now she was in the car, and she was showing me where to go. The conversation that took place inside the rental will forever live locked away in that little box of junk we'll never let our mothers hear.

This whole time I am thinking of Jesus.

She is scratching her arms almost violently and still smoking her cigarette. She's tweaking.

I'm trying to find out how much she's gonna charge for a blow-job.

She is rocking back and forth probably due to anxiety. Not from getting paid by a stranger to perform oral, but from the length of time it's been since she's gotten high. Maybe a few hours I assume. And still,...

I am thinking of Jesus.

She is telling me where to turn and I'm repeating it.

"Turn left" she says.

"Turn Left on 27th Avenue?" I enunciate well as if someone else is listening.

She tells me to turn down a small trail off of an even less traveled road. I realize there are nothing but trees around us which offer good cover.

A few minutes later, she's running into traffic to try and get away from me and I'm laughing in amusement as I half-heartedly chase her down.

She's screaming at me and crying and I can't help but laugh.

She makes it to a pay-phone and dials 9-1-1 before I can stop her.

A truck roars into the parking lot where the pay-phone is located and comes to a screeching halt as two police officers jump out. I grab the lady's arm and slam her to the ground, put hand-cuffs on her and tell her to stop resisting arrest.

I had just picked up my first prostitute for a sting operation, and I couldn't help but think about how this poor lady has ended up here.

*When I see what's happened to the young women in the city,*
*The pain breaks my heart.*
*Lamentations 3:51*
*The Message*

I could not help but think about how difficult it would be to share the love of Christ with her after I just spoke to her like she was nothing but a worthless piece of garbage. How difficult it would have been after making her believe, that me, allowing her to give me a blow-job for $40 is the best thing that will happen to her today.

Doesn't sound like your typical Christian book huh?

If this story is disturbing, it should be.

It's vulgar.

It's dirty.

It's abrasive.

Funny thing is, I've found that this is exactly where the church is. Not the corporate body of people who meet for worship on Sunday or the building in which they meet, but the kingdom. Where Jesus is trying to reach those lost in desperation and hopelessness.

The Sanctuary at my church is huge. It's clean, it's beautiful, it's cool, and inviting. I love it. I find refuge in my God, and when I enter that Sanctuary, my God has allowed me to be protected from all of the filth I am subject to each day. HE knows I need it and HE has allowed me to understand that I need to go to the Sanctuary as much as I can. I love that word: Sanctuary. Sometimes all I have to do is say the word and I am reminded of how good I feel when I go there and

I feel tons better. However, that isn't where the working prostitutes and dope-dealers are. That isn't where the lost are.

I often find it very difficult to walk such a very fine line. On one side of the balance, I am a husband, a father, a deacon at church, a basketball coach, a Sunday school teacher, and the founder of a non-profit organization designed to help soldiers and their families.

On the other side of the balance, I am a Deputy Sheriff who picks up prostitutes, buys drugs, chases down violent criminals, deals with rapists and child molesters, and fatal accidents to name a few.

Most importantly, right smack-dab in the middle of both, I am a man designed to have a relationship with GOD. That is why I am here. That is the best evaluation of who, and what, I am.

*The only accurate way to understand ourselves is by what God is*
*and by what he does for us.*
*Romans 12:3*
*The Message*

So that is the starting point. Realizing we are here to have a relationship with God. Realizing the best way to define ourselves is that we are a creation of God, built to glorify Him.

These stories are written by a guy trying to be more like the person God created him to be. I am constantly searching for that balance between the guy who kicks everyone's ass, and the guy who shares the light of Jesus. Not to complain or whine because I may have had it worse than some; but to further illustrate the conviction behind a guy fully aware of God's presence throughout his entire life. I did have it a little worse than most of the people I know, but I had it better than most people I don't.

I have asked myself repeatedly, is my life history and the choices I've made concerning paths I've chosen and the creation of the current man I am, all unrelated, chaotic events that just seem to fit nicely together?

A child who grows up beaten by his or her parent or parents typically grows up to beat his or her own children.

A child who grows up to see his mother beaten by his father regularly, typically grows up to beat women.

Children raised by alcoholics or drug addicts are at higher risk of becoming the same.

How in the hell do we become what we hate?

We are products of our environment.

Or are we?

I know there are exclusive cases where one defeats the odds.

The not typical.

The ones without glory.

The one everyone has overlooked.

The one who has overcome the odds.

The not-typical, non-glorious average Joe who has overcome incredible adversity.

Maybe you know someone….

A soldier trying to forget the look in a dying man's eyes and the haunting high-pitched gasp for his last breath.

A cop whose daughter is sitting on his lap, and he's struggling to keep from thinking of the nine-year old little girl he spoke to at work the day before who was bouncing up and down as she described, in great detail, a sexual encounter she had with a forty-year-old man.

A single mom whose fifteen-year-old son has shown up to her work at three o'clock in the afternoon throwing up because he drank too much.

Parents who wonder why their daughter sliced her wrists.

Students who have faced a gunman in the halls of their school.

A family member who has been selling her body for crack.

This sucks.

God isn't going to just make it all just disappear.

Jesus said that he had come to start a fire and turn everything upside down. How can the man who gave me his life say he came to disrupt rather than smooth things over?

If God loves me, why are things so bad?

Here's why...

# The Clown Lamp

*Next I turned my attention to all the outrageous
violence that takes place on this planet—
the tears of the victims, no one to comfort them;
The iron grip of oppressors, no one to rescue the victims from them.
So I congratulated the dead who are already dead
instead of the living who are still alive.
But luckier than the dead or the living is the
person who has never even been,
who has never seen the bad business that takes place on this earth.
Ecclesiastes 4:1–3
The Message*

*Everybody's got a story, and* this is an attempt to explain how my life developed a heart and soul driven towards a patriotic desire to serve, and the need to protect those who could not protect themselves. Most importantly, it is designed to show how our Awesome God has had a plan for my life long before I ever had a clue.

It is not that God allows horrible things to happen to us.

He allows us to endure horrible things.

At about the age of two, my mother and father divorced, and my mother was forced to move hours away from our family for work as an EMT. She met a man named Fernand, and I would soon begin to believe he was the most evil human being on the face of the planet.

In the beginning, everything was great. We all grew to love him as a caring, loving father-figure. After they were married, my brother was the first to receive regular beatings. As I got a little older, I was introduced to them.

The first one I can remember was when I was six, and I was taking a bath. Fernand must have been a bit more pissed-off than usual because my mother was working and he was left with the responsibility of taking care of the kids. This night I think he was even more pissed off because the sun was setting in The West again. So he makes a dramatic entrance into the bathroom and says…

"Get out of the fucking bath tub."

"I haven't washed my hair." I replied.

"Well, I'll fucking do it."

He reached across me, and grabbed a shampoo bottle.

Not just any shampoo bottle, but the one that had been empty.

The one that every six year-old knows must be filled with water for some unknown reason.

The one that this lunatic fully expected to contain shampoo.

Enter problem one.

As he squirted water into his hand, my eyes closed in a "god-help-me" way, and opened just in time to see his hand shaking with anger, turn to a fist, and connect with my left temple.

Enter problem two. Newton's third law: "For every action, there is an equal and opposite reaction." The impact of his fist to my head caused my head to hit the ceramic soap dish mounted into the tiled shower wall, and it cracked.

I just broke the soap dish.

He grabbed me, yanked me out of the tub, and beat me as he dragged me out of the bathroom, down the hall, and nearly all the way to my room.

I learned there would be no winning with him. I couldn't change his mind, and I damn sure couldn't stop him.

I was six.

He was huge.

That was life, and through the eyes of a six-year-old, that was the way it was always gonna be.

The next installment of Fernand's child rearing prowess I regard as worse.

It wasn't long after the hygiene lesson, and I had climbed up a book shelf that was situated between two closets in my bedroom. I don't really remember why I climbed it, I just did what boys do I guess. My mother saw me, told me to get down, and never do it again. Fine. Now, Fernand wasn't there, but she must have told him about it, because the next morning, after she left for work, he came to my room, woke me up, and said, "Show me how you climbed the book shelf."

"Mom said I can't."

"Climb it...now."

"Yes-sir."

This was bad. The whole time I attempted the climb he was taunting me...

"Well, get the fuck up there. C'mon, you wanna fucking climb, then climb."

When I reached the top, he said, "Now stay there you fucking idiot."

Enter problem one.

It's morning. I just got up. I have to pee.

After a couple of hours, I really had to pee. After another hour or so, I couldn't hold it. I knew if I asked him if I could go to the bathroom, I would be beaten. So far that morning, he hadn't hit me. I didn't want to test him, and I damn sure didn't want to bring him in there, so...

I just sat there until I pissed myself.

Enter problem two.

After about another hour, this time sitting in my urine soaked superman pajamas on the top of a bookshelf, he came to my door.

"Get down." He pauses, angles his head with a puzzled look on his face and asked, "What the fuck is that?" pointing at the darker blue areas of my pajama bottoms.

"I peed."

"You're fucking nasty."

He grabbed me, yanked me off of the book-shelf, and beat me as he dragged me out of my bedroom, down the hall and into the presence of my brother and a neighborhood kid, David, who would be riding to school with my brother that day.

The entire way to my brother's school Fernand made fun of me. Not only did he make fun of me, he taunted David and my brother to do so as well. Although my brother engaged in the harassment, he seemed to have this nervous look on his face that I remember to this day. And his face is what I remember with greater detail than anything else that day, in that car. Through his laughter, I saw sadness. Maybe I didn't know it at the time, but I think my brother knew his time in Fernand's favor would be brief. Pretty soon, Fernand would be strongly encouraging me to make fun of my brother...and I'd bite.

There were other lessons my brother and I learned.

What happens when you leave sour milk in the fridge.

What happens when you don't eat the fat from lamb chops.

What happens when you use more than two squares of toilet paper.

What happens when you sweep leaves off of a patio, and you don't stop the trees from dropping more.

Every lesson was accompanied by a punch, a kick, or forceful contact with a rigid object.

If it didn't, he invented new ways of torturing us.

The most difficult story to write about Fernand is one I had no intention of including in this book. It wasn't until months after this chapter was written, did I find out it needed to be included.

It was the Lamb Chops Lesson.

At seven years old, I didn't really care for fat. I didn't really care for lamb chops for that matter, but it was the fat that made the task of eating a lamb chop extremely difficult. I was picking at it, trying to pull off small pieces of meat when Fernand said, "Stop picking at it and eat it."

"I don't like the fat," I replied.

I continued to pick.

Without warning, Fernand burst out of his chair and came at me screaming, "I told you to fucking eat it!"

With his left hand, he grabbed my hair and yanked my head back as far as it would go.

With his right hand, he grabbed the lamb chop and shoved it into my mouth, bone and all.

Shoving a fat-covered lamb chop in and out of my mouth and throat, back and forth, he screamed "eat it mother-fucker eat it!"

I was gagging, unable to breathe. I had to keep my mouth opened as widely as I could to try and get air which only enabled him to keep shoving it deeper and deeper into my mouth and throat.

"Fucking bite down, fucking bite down, fucking bite down" he repeated as he shoved.

My head kept flailing back and forth trying to stop it, but he was too strong.

When he stopped, he left the bone halfway down my throat,

and he walked back to his chair.

I pulled the bone out, ran to the bathroom, and began to throw up.

While I was throwing up, Fernand had followed me into the bathroom and started slapping me in the back of the head and grabbing the back of my neck forcing my head into the bowl of the toilet which was quickly filling up with pieces of lamp chop and milk.

I thought he was going to drown me.

He let me know what an ungrateful piece of worthless garbage I was for throwing up an expensive meal in which he worked very hard to prepare for us.

He said I ruined dinner.

*He will redeem their life from*
*Oppression and violence;*
*And precious shall be their blood in His sight.*
*Psalm 72:14*

So in the midst of all this, my life sort of pivots on one particular day. It was after the lesson on the perils of shampooing and shelf climbing, and before the dinner etiquette lesson.

One beautiful morning, I awoke to the most brilliant sunlight shining through my bedroom window. It was a Saturday I'm sure, and I remember the sunlight and how it illuminated the room. As I have recalled it in the past and even now, the sunlight seemed to cause everything in the room to give off a surrealistic radiance.

What my eyes opened to, and what they focused on, was a lamp.

A small baby clown, painted in pastels. It was a friendly, inviting sculpture that had a light bulb that fit up inside and allowed just enough light to soak through the porcelain to give off a soft, steady glow.

As I stared into the eyes of the clown, I began thinking...

"What if this is it? What if this moment right now, is the rest of my life? One day, a long time from now, when I'm sixteen or something, I'm going to wake up right here, right now. Back in this bed, at this age, living in this house...and living with Fernand."

I didn't know if I could get up and I didn't want to. I wanted to stay in the bed and figure out how I would know that the rest of my life was not going to be nothing but a dream. I figured one day, when I'm grown up, I'm gonna have a great life and then wake up to this clown lamp, and nothing will have changed for me. I was afraid. I couldn't stand the thought of being subject to years of torture from Fernand, and then waking up one day, years after it was all over, only to return to his beatings and humility.

That day I did get up. I sat on the edge of my bed, and stared at the lamp for what seemed like an eternity.

The rest of the day I had a nervous, sick feeling in the pit of my stomach.

My recollection of that morning, the vision I had, and how I felt is very clear to me because I have often replayed it in my mind. At thirty-one, I sometimes wonder…what if?

Dreams in my adult life have found me waking up to that clown lamp, in that house.

So what does this have to do with being a follower of Christ?

Everything.

It has everything to do with a struggle that each and every person who reads this deals with everyday.

It has everything to do with my present day decision making.

My God has allowed me to return to that room, that morning, facing the image of that lamp which has become iconic to me regarding the beginning of a long and treacherous journey.

If I thought I had reached my fill of garbage already, that morning I would have slipped into insanity had I known all I was in for, over the next twenty-five years.

I'm sure glad God is smarter than me.

*Consider it a sheer gift, friends, when tests and challenges come at you from all sides.*
*You know that under pressure, your faith-life is forced into the open and shows its true colors.*
*So don't try to get out of anything prematurely. Let it do its work so you become mature and well-developed, not deficient in any way.*
*James 1:2–4*
*The Message*

# Beat It!

*After the years in Texas,* my mother, my brother, my sister and I moved in with my grandparents near Ft Lauderdale in Coral Springs. Everything seemed a little weird. Adam Walsh's abduction and death seemed to cast a shadow over the entire region that even a 7 year old could recognize. All conversation seemed to revolve around him, Michael Jackson, Drugs and this new MTV thing.

My mother cleaned houses during the day and operated a fork-lift at night. This meant that the three of us kids had a lot of time for mischief.

My mother must have realized we needed supervision after I torched a dumpster full of trash, so she finally enrolled us at the Boy's Club while my sister went to a sitter. Hanging out at the Boy's Club really wasn't much better of an option. Actually, thinking back, it may have been worse. I know that the boy's club is designed to prevent kids from getting into trouble, and today, it is a great program. However, in a poor neighborhood, with four-hundred misfit children congregating at the same place while mixing high-schoolers with middle and elementary aged children with minimal supervision, it has the susceptibility for bad things to happen.

There was a lot of fighting…

cursing,

stealing,

fighting,

drugs,

sex,

and of course there was plenty of fighting.

For some of us, as bad as it was at the boy's club, it was an escape from the outside. I was tired. I wanted dearly to find an escape from what seemed confusing: My life.

My mother didn't make a lot of money so we didn't live in the nicest of neighborhoods. The bigger kids always wanted to see the younger kids fight. So there I was. My brother fed me to them quite a few times to keep from getting his ass-kicked.

One day, during one of my bouts, I was doing quite well. During the fight I grabbed a kid by the arm and slung him to the ground. The older kids thought that was "bullshit".

"You do it again, and he gets free licks" they condemned.

Well, a few seconds later it happened again. Two guys grabbed me by the arms and told the kid to take his shots. The kid refused. They told him either "you take 'em, or we do it to you."

He took his shots.

Unfortunately, I took a hit that changed me forever.

It all started with Fernand's anger. When he punched me while I was in the bath-tub, I sustained an injury to my left ear.

This kid I was fighting punched me with everything he had, right in my left ear.

That was the day I started losing my hearing.

I cried when it happened. Mostly because it hurt. Partly because I just didn't want to do it anymore.

That was the first time in my life I remember wishing I could fight.

I thought about beating the kid that beat me. I thought about beating the kids that forced me into the fight. I thought about beating my brother for not standing up to the bigger kids. I wanted to beat the shit out of everyone. I just couldn't take the beatings anymore. Not only that, I couldn't take the fact that there was nothing I could do about it or that there was *no one to help me.*

So it began. I was totally beaten. Defeated. I had no one to turn to.

I even got in trouble when I got home that day. My mother was actually there and yelled at me for getting into a fight. She told me she had enough to worry about and that we were just making her life more complicated by putting her through this "shit".

"...I don't need this right now Ben. Your father didn't send the child support check this month so I have more important things to worry about right now if you don't mind."

No one.

At this point, I had NO ONE.

I went to my room and laid on my bed.

I cried for quite some time and stared at my Michael Jackson poster. He was wearing that big red leather jacket. You know the one he wore in the "Beat It!" video.

I started thinking of the song. I tapped my foot to the music playing in my head.

"Beat It!"

*Just beat it, beat it, beat it, beat it*
*No one wants to be defeated*
*Showin' how funky and strong is your fight …*
*It doesn't matter who's wrong or right*

You know, he sure did get those guys to stop fighting in the video.

Michael Jackson could help.

In the 'Beat It!' video, Michael Jackson is laying on his bed just like I am. He looks troubled in the video. I am troubled.

Michael Jackson would be my friend.

Beat it! The song played over and over in my head. All I could do is think about me and MJ taking on the whole neighborhood. That afternoon, Michael Jackson and I beat up all of the bullies, druggies, gang-bangers, my brother, and that kid who punched me in my ear. All the while, pausing momentarily to bust a quick dance move in between punches.

Michael Jackson was there for me.

Michael Jackson was someone I could look up to. I could feel it.

If I just do what Michael does, I'll turn out okay.

*They're out to get you, better leave while you can*
*Don't wanna be a boy, you wanna be a man*
*You wanna stay alive, better do what you can*
*So beat it, just beat it*

Is there anything Michael Jackson can't do? I bet he could fight monsters.

Wait a minute…he does, I've seen the video.

I've got a friend in MJ.

Sounds crazy doesn't it?

But isn't it true?

Just as I was a boy looking for comfort through Michael Jackson, children, teens, and adults are finding that same shelter in the latest figure in today's ICONIC culture.

The average American sees more than 3,000 advertisements per day. I am most definitely an average American when it comes to the observation of advertising. There it all is. They tell us what to eat, what to wear, how to look, how to feel, where to go, what to see, where to be, when to be, how to be, and what we need. They tell us that they are actually our friend. Nice touch.

This is incredible competition for God.

If that's not enough, everything is centered around...

You.

Not God.

You, you, you.

What you want.

How you want.

When you want.

Where you want.

Our culture tells us that we deserve better because life is hard. We deserve more. We deserve a dream job because we don't deserve having to listen to someone tell us what to do. We deserve an expensive meal because life is hard. We deserve a vacation because life is stressful. We deserve a better car because, I'm not making this up, with everything else going wrong in our life, at least we'll enjoy our ride to the job we hate. We deserve to buy what we want, eat what we want, say what we want, have sex when we want and with whom we want, and not have to take responsibility for it. We deserve to do drugs without being harassed. We deserve to defile ourselves and our lives to no limit and not have to be discriminated against, picked-on, scolded, or mocked because "that is the way I am, and I have to be me."

I'm free to be me.

Exactly.

People say it everyday.

Then they get pissed at God because their life isn't going the way they think it should.

Wonder why we get lost? We have everything in the world telling us about life.

Think of an advertising slogan.

Right now.

Make a list of all the advertisement slogans, sayings, tag-lines, jingles, or quotes from commercials you've seen.

Now make a list of all the scripture you know.

The world's got a bigger list, huh?

Mine too.

*It wasn't so long ago that you were mired in that old stagnant life of sin. You let the world, which doesn't know the first thing about living, tell you how to live. You filled your lungs with polluted unbelief, and then exhaled disobedience. We all did it, all of us doing what we felt like*

*doing, when we felt like doing it, all of us in the same boat. It's a wonder God didn't lose his temper and do away with the whole lot of us. Instead, immense in mercy and with an incredible love, he embraced us. He took our sin-dead lives and made us alive in Christ. He did all this on his own, with no help from us! Then he picked us up and set us down in highest heaven in company with Jesus, our Messiah.*
*Ephesians 2:1-6*
*The Message*

Ever wonder why we don't hear God talking to us?

When I was laying on my bed that day in Ft Lauderdale, I truly believed that Michael Jackson was singing that song about my life.

Michael Jackson was reaching out to me.

MTV reached out to me.

It's all reaching out to us. Not so that you or I will become better people, but so we will spend our money.

In Ft. Lauderdale in the early eighties, the world was reaching out to a kid who desperately needed to be reached. Unfortunately, I was being reached by the wrong message.

God reached out to me too. One day I was forced to go to church with one of my mother's friends. The only thing I can say about that experience was that during my visit, I received one of the coolest things ever: A tiny little red book which read "Holy Bible". It was about an inch square and had about ten pages. What was written inside, I have no clue. I do remember thinking that it was "cool" enough to take it to school for show and tell on Monday.

In the middle of my presentation, one kid asked me, "What book is it?"

"The Bible" I replied.

"No, what book is it?"

"The Bible."

"What book of the Bible is it?"

"It's just the Bible, I don't understand what you're saying."

"Never mind."

Everyone was looking at me like I was crazy. I had no idea that "The Bible" was made up of many different books. I had no idea what any of the Bible had to do with me or anyone else. The stories I had heard were mere fantasy to me. Fairy-tales which seemed as far-fetched as Greek Mythology. No one had ever taken the time to explain what was in the Bible. That experience was the closest I would come to having anything to do with God or the Bible for many years. I was right on the verge of knowing Christ and...

then, later on after school, it was back to the Boy's Club.

Boy George, Duran Duran, and The Clash, they were speaking much louder than God.

I don't know what I did with that Bible after that. I couldn't understand it. The Clash was cool, (they still are) and God, in my world, at that time was invisible (to many, he still is).

All I had to turn to that day on my bed was the world around me. As I look back on how I previously described the world around me at that age, the outlook for the rest of my life didn't look too good.

I have gone back to that day a thousand times. I wish I could go there as I am now. I don't wish I could prevent the fight from happening. I don't wish I could protect him from the outside world and the culture into which he was putting so much hope. I wish I could embrace that little boy and assure him everything was going to be just fine. I wish I could tell him about Jesus. I wish I could teach him that The Bible is God's promise to us that we can trust in him, and everything will be just fine in the end. I wish I could tell that little boy that I love him.

Now that I think about it,

I can.

*And don't be wishing you were someplace else or with someone else.*
*Where you are right now is God's place for you.*
*Live and obey and love and believe right there.*
*1 Corinthians 7:17*
*The Message*

# To Tame a Land

*After moving around Ft. Lauderdale* and Coral Springs, we all moved back to my home town in North West Florida. My mother met a guy named Bert at a little get-together hosted by friends of my mother's friend. I don't remember much about that first encounter but I do recall when he showed up at our apartment to take my mother on a date. My mother was running late as usual, so I answered the door. He was wearing shorts, flip-flops and a denim button-up short-sleeve shirt…and he was drinking a beer out of a can.

The first thing I noticed however was his smile. He had the look of a man who seemed he could be your best friend and greatest ally. His voice was soft, and his demeanor exuded confidence.

I smiled back and invited him in. As he walked in, he looked around, as if to inspect the condition of our living which was somewhat cramped, but clean. He made himself at home not completely from my prompting but from his relaxed sort of attitude.

I reported to my mother who was putting on her fifth outfit which was a black cocktail dress.

"What is he wearing?" she asked with urgency.

"He's in flip-flops and shorts Mom."

Her eyes got big and closed as she let out a sigh of relief.

This was the beginning of an intense struggle I would deal with for years to come and I embraced it with arms wide-open.

Bert was a Merchant Marine who lived in New Orleans and frequented North Florida to spend time with friends. He would go to work on a ship for two or three weeks at a time and rush back to Milton to spend time with my mother. My sister and I loved him. We were always excited to see Bert when he came to visit as if he were one of our own parents. He seemed to enjoy being a part of our family. My grandparents loved him and so did everyone else that met him. Bert had no family. His mother and father were never mentioned, and his "son" from a previous marriage he rarely spoke of, and never spoke to.

We became Bert's family.

He and my mother were in love. They had a great relationship. He treated her very well, and I had never seen my mother happier. One aspect of their relationship I enjoyed was, with Bert around, I didn't have to be the "man of the house".

He was fun to be around, extremely likable, and he always had a quick comeback with a wonderful sense of humor. When he walked into a room, everyone wanted to talk to him.

A few months after he and my mother started dating, he proposed.

My mother said yes.

My mother asked what my sister and I thought about it, and we enthusiastically gave her our blessing.

One day, after their decision to get married, they got into a fight. The argument lasted for hours. It started in the morning and by mid-afternoon, our neighbors who in an apartment complex were only a wall away, had a pretty good idea as to what was going on. One curious spectator in particular, was a soldier in the Army who was visiting his mother who lived next door. He was standing outside his mother's front door smoking a cigarette, listening to the loud thumps on the walls, and asked me about it as I sat on the curb in front of the apartment.

"He's not hitting her is he?"

"No." I lied. I was pretty sure I knew that Bert was pushing her around, and I was pretty sure that this jack-ass knew what was going on too. So he says…

"Well he had better not, 'cause I won't put up with that."

He flicked his cigarette to the ground, mashed it out with his toe, and went back inside away from the sounds of a body being slammed against the walls and furniture.

"What an asshole." I muttered, as he shut the door behind him.

I had no place to go. As mentally and physically uncomfortable as the curb may have been, I didn't want to be any further from my mother. I realized I wasn't going to do anything; I was too scared to even say anything. I couldn't protect her, but I couldn't leave her.

I just sat there.

"What an asshole." I thought, as I dreamt of what I should and could be doing, but knew I wouldn't.

Later on that afternoon, Bert left for New Orleans for work, and someone finally called the Sheriff's Office. A female deputy came out to the house, spoke with my mother briefly, and left. That was it. My mother talked about leaving, but decided it would be best to stick it out and try and make it work. I shamefully recall that I thought that was the best idea and I let her know.

We began to see another side of Bert. He was still funny and likable enough to make everyone think that the fight was just an isolated incident and would never happen again. However, his occasional door slamming and frying pan hurling kept us on our toes. More and more, a monster emerged. Worse yet, we learned that his entire lifestyle up to this point had revolved around learning to hurt people.

My mother went to New Orleans to help Bert pack his house for the move to Florida, and came back with tales of how his entire house was set up for martial arts training. Focus pads, boxing gloves, and martial arts magazines littered the apartment. His living room was adorned with a speed bag mounted to the wall, and a heavy-bag mounted to the ceiling. An inflatable leather bag in one corner was attached by rope from the top of the bag to the ceiling, and by bungee cord from the bottom to the floor designed to increase speed and accuracy. Burt's collection of martial arts weaponry rivaled that of any Kung-fu movie, which he also had a collection of. Of course, I was thirteen and fascinated by this. What thirteen year old wouldn't love an instant martial arts studio? I did, and when I eagerly approached him to teach me to fight, I could tell that his desire to have a protégé was as strong as my desire to learn. Bert was going to teach me to fight. I was going to learn to "annihilate" or "cripple" my opponents as Bert so often put it.

He and my mother married, we moved into a house, and the garage was set up for training. Our "lessons", usually consisted of him forcing me to punch and kick the heavy bag a few hundred times, work the speed bag, and him kicking my ass. The whole time I'm listening to him regurgitate and stammer through Chinese Philosophy.

All the while, he and my mother got along pretty well after they were married with a few bouts here and there.

One day, I had a run in with a neighborhood kid. I didn't want to fight him and despite his insistence, I backed down. So this kid's father comes out of his house as I'm walking away and gets a very wrong version of what happened from his son.

He comes after me, and I froze.

Upon his approach he informs me that I was white trash and didn't know who I was "fucking with." He let me know that this was his neighborhood, and I had better watch my step or he'll have my ass. I try and tell him what happened and he says...

"Shut your god-damned mouth and get the fuck out of here."

I immediately went home and nearly walked into Bert standing akimbo as I entered the front door. Bert had been watching from across the street, inside the house, the whole time.

"What was that all about?" he asked, with a very stern look.

I told him the whole story and he listened carefully. I tried to explain to him that I really had not done anything wrong and he told me "I don't give a shit if you did anything wrong or not."

He walked to the fridge, pulled out a beer, opened it and slowly took a sip and said...

"Well, let's go have a talk with him."

I asked if I could stay home and he told me no. He assured me I needed to see "this".

So I lag behind as Bert crosses the street and I'm praying the guy isn't home anymore. Bert knocks on the door and the guy comes outside.

"Can I help you?" he says.

"Yes-sir, you can. I'm Bert." as he puts his hand out for a shake.

The man tells his name and extends his hand, and the two shake.

Bert lets the guy know that it was all a misunderstanding.

The guy responds well and lets Bert know he doesn't want any trouble in the neighborhood between the kids.

Bert followed up with this:

"Well, you know, we're gonna be living across the street from each other for quite some time so I think we should get along. I think these boys should get along. But if you ever talk to my son like you did today, I'll beat your fucking head into the concrete."

Bert told him that I was a good kid and from now on it would be a good idea for him to get permission before he even said hello to me.

The guy apologized for the way he wrongfully treated me and told Bert there was no need for threats.

Bert assured him, it was no threat.

The guy assured Bert he would never do it again.

I had a new hero.

Later on that afternoon, Bert gave me a book he wanted me to read entitled "To Tame a Land". Although he told me he had, I don't believe he ever read it.

If he had, he wouldn't have given it to me.

The book was a Louis La'mour western that is basically about a kid who loses his father and spends some time with a man who teaches him about life, philosophy and how to fight. Later on, the kid grows up to become a Sheriff and ends up facing his nemesis which, in the final scene, he learns is his mentor from the past.

How prophetic.

Tuesday, April 2nd, 1991. It was my mother's birthday. Mom was working as a waitress at a popular bar & grill on the beach about forty-five minutes away from home. My sister and I got home and started our homework while being entertained by Bert.

"Ahhh, you guys can finish that later. Let's go for a ride."

Every kid loves to be told they don't have to do their homework. We dropped our pencils and ran to his car. We went to my Grandparent's house and visited for a little while. We stayed long enough for Bert to finish a couple of glasses of Bailey's Irish Cream. We rode back to the house, stopping along the way for a case of beer.

Once at the house, Bert wanted to train.

At first, I thought he was only playing.

After thirty minutes or so of him chasing me around the yard telling me to attack him with a psychotic look in his eyes, I figured he might be serious.

At one point, I was hiding on the opposite side of a privacy fence watching him through one of the cracks. He had been looking for me and going through some ridiculous kung-fu combat walk through the back yard and stopped. He slowly looked left, slowly looked right, and when his eyes caught mine, he froze.

Standing in the middle of the back yard in a combat stance, he stared at me.

This could be serious.

The sound of my mother's car pulling into the driveway returning from work broke the moment. I ran to her car and pretended nothing seemed a little odd about Bert this evening. She had brought home pizza, and the four of us quickly gathered around the table to eat. Bert began making jokes at my mother's expense, and when she let him know that she didn't approve, he began chastising her for getting home so late. He was angry at her because there wasn't a whole lot of time left to celebrate her birthday. So my mother walked out to her car and returned with a birthday cake in her arms. She dropped it on the table and said...

"This is what I spent my tips on so you and the kids could have cake on my birthday."

What a cool mom.

She actually figured that my sister and I would enjoy having cake on her birthday, so for no other reason, she bought herself a birthday cake.

She walked into her bedroom on the opposite end of the house, and shut the door behind her.

Bert sat back in his chair with a smile.

He had been beaten in this argument, and I was amused.

"Mom sure showed him," I thought.

I just wish I had kept my thoughts to myself and my mouth shut. What I said next, I always wished I hadn't. For years, I felt like the comment I made sitting at that dinner table with Bert and Amanda triggered a very significant change in that chapter of our lives.

"I guess your name is 'dirt'. I bet that stung." I said with a smirk.

Bert smiled at me and nodded. He sighed, wiped his mouth with his napkin, took a sip of beer, and excused himself from the table.

A short time later he returned and his right arm was wet.

He sat down at the table, dried his arm with a hand-towel, and took another bite of pizza. He sipped his beer and said smiling, "Yep, I guess I really screwed up for her birthday."

What Amanda and I didn't know, was that Bert walked into the bedroom, entered the bathroom, reached into the shower and grabbed my mother's throat and while choking her said, "Don't you ever talk to me like that again you fuckin' bitch or you'll never make it to your next fuckin' birthday."

After dinner, my sister and I took turns taking a shower and when I was partially dressed my mother came into my room and said, "We're leaving tonight, don't go to sleep."

Bert stormed into the room and said "what the fuck are you doing?"

"I'm talking to my son." she replied.

"What the fuck are you saying to him?"

"It's none of your business. Let me speak to my son alone."

"Fuck that. We're a family, you got something to say then say it."

"Bert, let me talk to mom," I nervously interjected.

Bert left the room and my mother started where she left off.

"Sleep lightly; we're leaving as soon as he passes out."

I shut out the light, and lay in my bed.

I was a million miles away from anyone.

I was afraid. I was afraid for my mother. I was afraid he would kill us if he caught us leaving. I kept wishing she wouldn't wake me up to leave that night. At that point, I didn't know anything had really happened. All I knew was that Bert was drunk, and he was acting like an ass. "Big deal" I thought. "What's new?"

It was then I heard a sound that makes me nervous every time I think about it. It makes me nervous thinking about it right now, as a grown man.

The sound was distinctive. Not like something you hear on a daily basis and can easily identify with, but in context, and coupled with obscure meaningless curses afterward, told me something that stunned me motionless.

It was the sound of my mother being choke-slammed into her bedroom door. I could tell it was near the top of the door, and in my mind I could almost see her feet dangling. I could hear choking sobs, and Bert throwing every curse word he knew at her.

My mom was having the life choked out of her.

I froze.

I did nothing.

I didn't even call the police.

I laid there, motionless.

Chills from head to toe, I felt literally frozen.

"Worthless coward," I thought.

When I heard her slide down the door and Bert walk away, I breathed. I was relieved for two reasons: One, he didn't kill my mother, and two, I didn't have to worry about doing anything.

"Spineless coward."

The rest of the night, I awoke every hour or so. I would rise up in my bed, listen for a moment, and when I was sure all was quiet and everyone was asleep, I would lay back down and fall asleep disbelieving this night was actually happening.

The next morning, my mother drove us to school before Bert got out of bed. After that night, the only time I ever saw him again was in depositions.

He went to jail that day, and during the investigation, someone discovered his ex-wife in New Orleans. I saw the pictures of a woman beaten in the face so badly her lips were disfigured and there wasn't a spot on her face that wasn't purple and lacerated. There were two or three bald spots on her head from chunks of hair being yanked out. The maestro of that beating was Bert. My mother was lucky from a certain point of view. Aside from bruising around the neck, wrists and back, she was fine.

That day at school, I only spoke to my girlfriend about the incident. She always told me about how her daddy used to beat her momma all the time before he left her for another woman. It made me sick. I didn't know if I was gonna have to get used to doing nothing about the violence, or if I would inevitably have to take action.

For years I carried that night around on my shoulders.

The following summer, while visiting my father and brother who lived about six hours away, my brother started in.

He and my father and I were sitting at the table eating dinner and the conversation about that night came up. My brother said, "You know what Ben? I'm pissed at you because you were there and heard Bert beating her ass and you didn't do anything."

I don't remember crying but I wanted to.

It hurt…

because it was true.

Now I knew what my father and my brother were thinking.

I felt pathetic.

I felt like a physically weak, spineless coward.

*He delivered me from my strong enemy,*
*From those who hated me,*
*For they were too strong for me.*
*They confronted me in the day of my calamity,*
*But the Lord was my support.*
*Psalm 18:17-18*
*NKJV*

I wondered if my mother felt the same way about me. Turns out, my mom and dad walked around with their own demons. They felt even worse than I did. Not just for everything that happened with Bert, but for everything. Everything that happened to my brother and my sister and I. The abuse, Fernand, South Florida,…everything. It wasn't until I had children of my own until I truly understood that.

When my son was an infant, the first time I found out he could roll over was when he rolled off of the couch and on to the floor. He landed with a thump. That was the first thing I heard. The second was his cry. It was not the "I'm hungry" cry. It wasn't the "I'm tired", or the "I'm wet" cry. It was the "I'm in pain" cry that every parent knows. When I picked him up, his little baby arms were stretched out, hands in a claw like form shaking back and forth, and he was screaming so hard his face looked as if it would explode. I realized I was shaking too.

I felt so horrible. I felt like it was my fault. I didn't know he had been rocking back and forth, but I still felt like it was something I should have prepared for. I wanted to throw the couch off of the balcony. I needed to be mad at something. I needed something on which to blame my son's pain. Something on which to blame my pain. That was just because my son fell off of the couch. I can't imagine how I would feel if he had to experience what I had.

For years, my parents walked around with that weight on their shoulders.

The day my son fell off of the couch, he began to learn what it's like to fall. He also began to learn what it's like for him to be picked up by his father. My parents have had to watch me fall, and they have had to watch me writhe in pain.

Each and every time I have done so, I have been picked up by my *Father.*

Like an infant, I just didn't know until years later.

*Distress that drives us to God does that.*
*It turns us around. It gets us back in the way of salvation.*
*We never regret that kind of pain.*
*But those who let distress drive them away from God are full of regrets,*
*end up on a deathbed of regrets.*
*2 Corinthians 7:10*
*The Message*

# Gain

*When I was in High* school, my sister Amanda and I lived with my mother in Northwest Florida, and my brother lived with my father in Central Florida. I had been raising my sister for quite a few years at that point and was helping my mother the best I could. My mother and I got along pretty well. After all, we had been through a lot together.

The years in Texas and Coral Springs sort of took a back-seat to a whole new load of junk we had to deal with.

Our house had burned down two weeks before Christmas which had us moving in and out of motels and into an apartment complex with more rough kids and bad influence.

Sadly, I think at this point, I may have been the bad influence. Aside from the smoking, arson, theft, destruction, cursing and fighting…I was a nice kid.

After a couple of moves here and there, we moved into a house on the beach with a couple of roommates.

…and then there was Jason.

Jason was my height, my age. We had the same blonde hair, same blue eyes, and same demeanor.

I met Jason when I started taking the 45 minute bus ride from the new house to my high-school. We shared a few classes together but rarely said anything to each other at first.

Jason and I didn't get along very well in the beginning. He made a comment that bothered me in the middle of one of our classes so, in front of the teacher and everyone I slapped him across his face. He just sat there dumbfounded.

One day soon after, we were best friends.

It happened just as simple as that.

By the time he and I cleared the ninth-grade, we had become prodigal members of each other's family.

I began to love him as if he were my own brother.

If you saw one, you saw the other. People began to make jokes about how he and I were stuck to each other and we'd just respond by telling them to go and do something vulgar to themselves.

I switched high-schools between the 10th and 11th grade, and Jason lasted two days at our old high school before he followed. We only worked where the other could work, and after we quit the third restaurant we worked at together, we were pretty sure no one in that entire city would hire the two of us together ever again.

Jason and I even attempted to join the Marine Corps together. He got accepted and was given a date to ship out. I got a letter saying I would never be eligible for military service due to a heart condition I didn't have. Recruiting for the military wasn't a problem then so denials came pretty easily with hardly any basis for said denial.

I descended rapidly after that. I had been planning a military career since I was a child. Now, the one thing I counted on in life wasn't going to happen.

The smell of perfume and gasoline didn't help either.

I went from being an honor student to an "F" student who had more absences at school than days present.

Jason stuck with me.

Jason's Mom and Dad, Beth and Jim, had become my Mom and Dad. Jason's sister Nic, had become my sister. For the most part, they stopped calling me Ben, and started calling me son. I started referring to them as Mom and Dad. It was the same for Jason and my parents.

So after four years of living, working, going to school, fully becoming a part of each other's life, and trying to completely destroy ourselves with cigarettes, alcohol, and girls, Jason and I graduated high school.

The summer after graduation, Jason left for Parris Island.

Not long after he left, I had a vision. Okay, maybe it wasn't a "vision", but it was definitely God speaking louder than the world through the foulest woman I had ever laid eyes on.

I was standing in a convenience store at about 5:30 in the afternoon when everyone was stopping to pick up their six-pack of beer to end their work day. The front page of the newspaper showed a picture of a military corpsmen (medic) giving an immunization to a child in Haiti. I was standing there thinking about how the Marines had landed in Haiti, and that Jason may someday be in combat without me.

My moment was interrupted by a woman standing next to me in line. She began loudly voicing her opinion about hard-working American tax-dollars paying for "niggers around the world" to receive medical treatment, referring to the same front-page at which I was staring. There were at least 20 people standing in the store. Shockingly, nearly all of them engaged in this conversation with her, to include the store clerk. All were repeating vile racial slurs that I couldn't believe I was actually hearing. I looked around and saw myself standing right there among them.

My vision?

"I'm gonna be standing in a convenience store 10 years from now with no shirt, covered from head to toe in sawdust and dirt from a low paying construction job buying a case of beer while having a conversation so ignorant it's idiocy would be unrivaled. I will have accomplished nothing."

*And so I insist—and God backs me up on this—*
*that there be no going along with the crowd,*
*the empty-headed, mindless crowd.*
*They've refused for so long to deal with God*
*that they've lost touch not only with God*
*but with reality itself.*
*They can't think straight anymore.*
*Ephesians 4:17*
*The Message*

Three days later I moved to my father's house, six hours away.

Jason ended up breaking his hip while in boot camp and on December 7th, 1995, I drove to Parris Island and picked him up to take him home. He was being discharged from the Marine Corps due to a hip problem he was going to have to deal with for the rest of his life.

When I arrived on Parris Island I was amazed. The temperature was low thirties yet everything still looked green. Everything was perfect. Meticulously manicured grass, pristine brass and metal accents along with the sound of cadence in the distance on an uncharacteristically dark day made me feel very uneasy. Of course, walking around the quintessential training base of the world's finest fighting force with more than shoulder length hair and an earring possibly added to my anxiety.

I knocked on a couple of squad-bay entry doors looking for Jason and was met with a man who looked as if he were chiseled from stone wearing a uniform that appeared to be made of concrete and steel. He was a Parris Island Drill Instructor and just his presence was intimidating. He very politely let me know that Jason was not ready to leave yet. The Drill Instructor directed me to the Post fast food joint and the Marine Corps Museum, and assured me Jason would be along shortly. When Jason finally found me, I was wandering through the Marine Corps Museum dreaming of what it would be like to be a Marine.

It felt like I hadn't seen him in an eternity. I could tell he had changed but to me, he was still Jason. I felt like he had grown up a little more than I had. Jason had always been a confident person, but now, his confidence exuded a natural power. Although he was discouraged he didn't make it through boot camp, I was proud of him.

The entire time we drove home, he was telling me boot camp stories which started stirring something inside me. After Christmas, I went to the Marine Recruiter and told him to forget the sales speech, "just get me in." The second week of January of 1996, I was miraculously allowed by the Department of Defense to enlist in the Marine Corps, and I was given a mid April date to ship out.

March 3rd, 1996, I was on a date with a girl from a church I had been attending, and as we walked out of the movie theater, adjacent to the Marine Recruiting office in a small plaza, one of my recruiters called me over. He was giving me the opportunity to become an "MP". The catch was, I had to leave the next morning for boot camp. It was about 10pm, and I had about ten minutes to decide.

After a quick phone call to my father who nervously agreed that this is what I had wanted, I hung up and told the recruiter…

"Let's do it."

I spoke to Jason for quite some time on the phone that night trying to pick up on any last minute tips and pointers on how to survive boot camp.

The next morning, I was on a bus headed for Parris Island.

# Marine

*"I said to myself, 'This is it. I'm finished. God is a lost cause."*
*Lamentations 3:18*
*The Message*

"*For those of you who* are just passing through, On behalf of the Base Commander, I want to welcome you to the Marine Corps Recruit Depot, Parris Island, South Carolina. I hope you enjoy your brief visit to the beginning of the world's finest fighting force. However, I do apologize if you are offended in any way by what you are about to witness."

"For those of you who have reached their destination, your journey has yet to even begin. When I give you the command to get off of my bus, you will quickly move your nasty behinds out of my seats, get your repugnant, filth ridden bodies off of this bus and proceed to the rear and stand on my yellow foot-prints."

I was smiling.

Screams emitted like cannon fire.

I'm not sure what he said at this point exactly, but he was not happy.

Next, I was standing on the infamous yellow foot-prints at the Parris Island, Marine Corps Recruit Depot, South Carolina.

And I was still smiling. This would be the last time I would smile for almost three months.

My Grandfather was a Marine. To me, he was, and still is, *The* Marine. He joined the Marine Corps out of Jackson, Mississippi at the age of seventeen. To hear him tell it, "there wasn't nothing' for an Irish kid in Jackson, so it was trouble or the Corps." He lied about his age, and at the age of eighteen found himself in the middle of a World War. The Asian campaign for the Marine Corps during World War II proved to be some of the Marines' finest moments. My Grandfather was a part of it. He was on the beginning of an Island hopping Campaign that left him on Corregidor, the last of a few strong-holds in the Philippine Islands, when it fell. After an attempt to swim halfway across the mouth of Manila Bay, my Grandfather ended up on the Island of Bataan.

Amazing.

He survived the infamous Bataan Death March and three and a half years later, he was released from prison camp. At twenty-one years old and eighty-five pounds, he was a free man.

While on leave, back home in Jackson, he met my Grandmother, Louise. A couple months later he simply said to her, "Louise, you're either gonna marry me or not. Either way kid, I'm leaving soon so you need to make up your mind."

My Grandfather stayed in the Marine Corps until retirement at the time of the Vietnam War. He earned a meritorious wartime commission to 2nd Lt during the Korean War, and started teaching at colleges soon after.

For years, I walked by a display case showcasing all of his decorations, and I never truly understood what all of it meant.

Now, here on Parris Island, I started to see it. I wouldn't truly understand for years to come, but the idea began to emerge.

I'm on Parris Island. I couldn't believe it.

I was happy…well, sort of. My hair was very blonde and very long, and I had been accustomed to running my fingers through it or pulling it back into a ponytail over and over. Now, after only three hours on this island, there is no hair, only stubble and skin.

Rubbing my head from curiosity elicited a completely unexpected response from a Drill Instructor who seemed to appear from no where:

"Rub your head one more time and I fucking kill you."

Well, I think he got his point across.

I was still happy.

All these years I wanted to be tough.

No more crying.

No more shying away from challenges.

No more talk about how fighting doesn't solve anything when I know I feel differently.

No more of the child-like dreams of me being a bad-ass.

No more of putting up with people's garbage…after boot camp was over of course.

No more being a coward.

And do you know what else?

No more beatings that I can't do a damn thing about. For me, my mother, my brother, my sister, or anyone else for that matter. I'm signing on to become a protector. *God wants* me to be a Marine. Becoming a Marine was *all I ever dreamed of.* If I could just reach that one goal, I'll have arrived. I'll be completely satisfied. I will have reached the plateau on top of the mountain I have been climbing for all these years. I will hunger no more. The fire inside will die. The guilt, the shame, the burden…all gone.

At least, that's what I thought.

But I was happy.

Welcome to the suck.

The Marine Corps is quite possibly the most fascinating organization known to man. Boot camp sucks. Life in the Marine Corps sucks most of the time because your Sergeants suck most of the time. The rules are asinine, childish and absurd, and they suck.

But don't ever say that to a Marine. Wanna strike up a conversation with one? Start off with "momma" jokes before you start talking badly about the Corps. Marines are fonder of the Marine Corps than most people are about anything. Think about it. No one gets a McDonald's tattoo after three months of working there. No one barks like a dog when you mention that you work for such and such company. And on November 10th, all across America, thousands of Marines are stopping for a beer at a local bar on the way home from work. Aside from December 25th and July 4th, the tenth of November may be the most celebrated birthday in America.

Why is it like this? Because of people like my grandfather. Because of people whose sacrifice resembled that of Christ's. Because no matter how bad, how selfish, or how hard-headed we believe the next generation is or is going to be, there are still those men and women, not only in the Marine Corps, but in all branches of the military, who decide to risk it all for the benefit of others. They dedicate their life to something bigger.

Yet there I was, getting told I was a worthless maggot who doesn't deserve to breath Parris Island air, so the idea that this will turn out somewhat glorious in the end has not yet been found.

But I'm still happy.

I am becoming a Marine.

I learn I amount to nothing. I will make no facial expressions. I will show no emotion. I learn how to put on my trousers and blouse. My bootlaces will be left over right with a bridge. Bulkheads, decks, mug jars, mote tables, moonbeams, go-fasters, portholes, pie-holes, and ink-sticks. I am drinking water. I learn to live with my fists clenched tightly at all times. I am a cheating maggot who is not giving 100%. I try harder. Jody, Suzy, bag-nasties, bivouc, quarter-decks and emergency head-calls with lights and sirens. I will not bounce while marching. I will take 120 steps per minute. I will lean back and my fingers will, for the rest of my life, brush along the seams of my trousers while walking with my fists still clenched tightly. Six to the front, three to the rear. I am a derelict piece of shit who still isn't giving 100%. One shot one kill. Sight-alignment, sight-picture. I learn that what actually makes the grass grow is blood. Bright red blood. I stop taking the easy way. I start asking for the hard way. I am now giving 100%, which still isn't enough so I must become more of who I am. Not for me, but for other Marines. For the U.S. I am becoming stronger. I change. I am confident. I realize that no one can tell me I can't do something. If they do, choke them. I will allow no one to oppress or harm others. If they do, kill them. I am the most powerful weapon on the planet. I am a Marine.

This is my rifle.
There are many like it, but this one is MINE.
My rifle is my best friend.
It is my life.
I must master it as I must master my life.
My rifle without me is useless.
Without my rifle, I am useless.
Excerpt from:
*The Rifleman's Creed*
-Major General William H. Rupertus, USMC-

The day of graduation I feel extraordinary.

*He ground my face into the gravel.*
*He pounded me into the mud.*
*I gave up on life altogether.*
*I've forgotten what the good life is like.*
*I said to myself, "This is it. I'm finished.*
*GOD is a lost cause."*
*Lamentations 3:16–18*
*The Message*

So often in our lives, we see exactly where we want to be. Where we will be happy.

"If I can just make it there, I will be satisfied."

"I will hunger no more."

This is where hope is more like wishful thinking.

Up to this point in my life, I prayed that God would make me strong. I prayed that I would someday stop being the victim, and start being the hero. I knew that somehow, some way, God would change me into the kind of man I always wanted to grow up and be. It was my dream for so long that I took for granted what God allowed me to do. I became a Marine. I became strong in mind and body. I now knew there was nothing I couldn't accomplish. I found the philosophy that where ability and talent end, intensity begins. I felt as if there was nothing stronger than my mind as a Marine. In a way, I was right. What I did with it, was wrong.

God's plan was amazing. I look back and realize I had taken a very worldly mindset on how my life was going to turn out. I envisioned a guy who would one day save the world like Rambo. I ate, slept, and lived the Marine Corps, and I slowly drifted further and further away from God: from Him, His word and His plan.

It probably looked less like drifting and more like sprinting away from God.

I felt like I had finally become what I always wanted to be without God's help. The way it looked to me was that I took matters into my own hands, and I finally started to get things done. I started to see that God's plan didn't really fit with what I thought was the Marine Corps' plan. I sinned. I became a cliché. I was the poster child for a hard-charging, do-or-die, smoking, drinking, cursing, sex-crazed, little bad-ass Marine.

The more I sinned, the more I wanted to sin.

The more I wanted to sin, the more I justified it.

I buried myself deeper and deeper into sin. The more I sinned, the more I buried myself.

I was trying to hide from God.

In the book of Genesis, God decides to make man. God made Adam and "set him in down in the Garden of Eden to work the ground and keep it in order." *Genesis 2:15, The Message.*

*God commanded the Man, "You can eat from any tree in the garden, except from the Tree-of-Knowledge-of-Good-and-Evil.*
*Don't eat from it. The moment you eat from that tree, you're dead."*
*Genesis 2:16-17,*
*The Message.*

So God creates woman and they both live in the Garden together. They felt no shame. They had a personal relationship with God. They were with God. They were routinely exposed to his glory. They were living as God intended for them (us) to live.

Then Satan comes into the Garden. Well, actually it was a snake. The Bible never really tells us that it was Satan, but by his work we know that this is no ordinary snake.

An image of the rest of our lives begins right here.

Satan causes confusion in Eve's heart. God may not have told Eve directly not to eat from the "tree of life". What we do know is that he told Adam. But by Eve's response to the snake, we must assume that she was told.

Satan asks Eve if God told them

*"...not to eat from any tree in the Garden?"*
*The Woman said to the serpent, "Not at all.*
*We can eat from the trees in the garden.*
*It's only about the tree in the middle of the garden that God said,*
*'Don't eat from it; don't even touch it or you'll die.'"*
*The serpent told the Woman, "You won't die.*
*God knows that the moment you eat from that tree,*
*you'll see what's really going on.*
*You'll be just like God, knowing everything,*
*ranging all the way from good to evil."*
*Genesis 3:2–5*
*The Message*

Slowly we want to go our own way. We want to take control of our life. We get tired of knowing we aren't in charge. Eve begins to wonder if she can be like God.

So what did Eve really have to be unhappy about?

Nothing.

That was most likely the problem.

What did I have to be angry about as a Marine in Okinawa? I did whatever I wanted with my body. I did whatever I wanted with my soul. I wasn't getting beaten down anymore. I didn't have to worry about being able to protect myself. After all, fighting turned into an extracurricular activity in the Marine Corps. It was fun.

When things are going our way, and everything seems right in our life, we forget who made it so.

Then we walk away.

We thank God when our lives are in that realm opposite hard-ship in what we have come to term "blessed".

Then we walk away.

There's Eve. There's Adam. There's the fruit. They're doing just fine without God. Who needs him. It's not like they need medical care. They don't need jobs to pay the bills. They don't need insurance. They don't even need a house.

So they eat.

Their eyes are opened, and they feel shame.

They *knew* they were naked.

They tried to make clothes for themselves. I guess the fig-leaf wardrobe didn't quite measure up because when Adam and Eve heard "God strolling in the garden in the evening breeze", they hid.

They were going to be exposed to God's glory with their new "eye-sight", and they were afraid.

God called to the Man: 'where are you?'

He said, "I heard you in the garden and I was afraid because I was naked. And I hid."

God knew where Adam was. God knows where each of us is. He is omnipresent. No matter how clever it sounds, we are not looking for God. We are not looking for Jesus. I can't ask, "Have you found Jesus?" A more appropriate question would be "have you allowed yourself to stop trying to hide from God?"

We bury ourselves in our sin. The more we sin, the more we try and cover ourselves up with it to hide from God. We get angry at God because he is so perfect. We don't compare.

I made excuse after excuse and tried like hell to justify as to why I was doing what I was doing.

Over the years I remained a Godless wretch.

During a year-long tour in Okinawa, I met the sweetest, most beautiful young lady I have ever seen. Her name was Lavonne, and she was a Marine. She lived and enlisted in the Marine Corps in a town about forty-five minutes from where I lived and enlisted.

Just over a year after we met, we were married, living in Washington, D.C, and had a son we named Ben.

I didn't think I could be happier until fifteen months after my son was born, we had a baby girl we named Gladys.

We lived very happily in Washington until the end of my enlistment, at which time we all moved to Florida where I was to pursue a civilian law enforcement career.

About three days after my last Marine Corps paycheck, I received a letter from a police department thanking me for applying with their agency. "However, we regret to inform you…" followed, and let me know that I was not going to get the job, and I was now unemployed.

Two months later, my wife and kids and I were broke and homeless.

I continued to believe I was keeping myself hidden from God. My wife and I both continued to bury ourselves deeper and deeper into sin.

*Everything I wanted I took–I never said no to myself.*
*I gave in to every impulse, held back nothing.*
*I sucked the marrow of pleasure out of every task–*
*my reward to myself for a hard day's work!*
*Then I took a good look at everything I'd done,*
*looked at all the sweat and hard work.*
*But when I looked, I saw nothing but smoke.*
*Smoke and spitting into the wind.*
*There was nothing to any of it.*
*Nothing.*
*Ecclesiastes 2:9–11*
*The Message*

# Loss

"Jason's had an accident at work."

I was trying to listen to my mother tell me what has happened to the guy I loved as dearly as I loved anyone but my hand began trembling and I hung up. I was at my father's office when I got the call and as I hung up I ran out the door and headed home to pack a bag. I had worked from midnight to eight in the morning and received the call at about 9am. On no sleep, I was headed back to my hometown within a couple of hours.

Jason had been working at a high-rise construction site the previous day when he fell three stories and separated his aorta from his heart. Witnesses say he jumped up after landing on his face and chest and tried to walk it off. Somehow, he kept surviving. When he was brought into the trauma center at a hospital in Pensacola by helicopter, a renowned heart surgeon leaving the hospital for home decided to see if there was anything he could do. He ended up keeping Jason alive by grafting the aorta back to the heart and massaging Jason's heart with his hand to keep it pumping.

Jason's wife and parents greeted me when I arrived that afternoon, and I was expecting the worst. However, I received good news. Jason was surviving. Though incoherent, swollen, bruised, scraped, bandaged, and hooked up to every machine imaginable, he was alive.

So I stayed strong for everyone. Although I felt like I was dying inside, I never allowed myself to show my pain around anyone. Whenever I was alone with him I just sat and held his hand the best I could, without hurting him. Sometimes he would wince in pain when touched which was actually encouraging considering the severity of the accident.

The second day, I made him smile, and I knew he was going to survive. Jason amazed everyone. The doctors didn't believe that Jason could respond to me when I would ask him to open his eyes until I showed them. Jason was still able to respond to language; a function the doctors thought Jason would have lost due to the trauma to the brain. He was getting incredibly better each day. He was still not very awake, and due to the bones in his face and jaw being shattered he couldn't talk. Subtle tilts of the head indicated "yes" and "no". Eyes straining to open only a slither and a slight squeeze of the hand or wiggle of the toes indicated he knew we were there, and he was gonna be fine.

Jason's Father-in-law and pastor ensured him that Jesus would see him through this. As out of touch with a meaningful relationship with God as I was, I agreed. Jason had just recently become a Christian, a fact that has since made this story glorious.

After a couple of weeks, Jason was doing really well, and I went home to spend some time with my wife and children with plans to return after a couple of days. Our Dad, Jim, left Beth at the Hospital and flew back to California where he and Beth had been living so he could take care of a few things as well.

The day after I came home, a counselor from the Hospital called.

Jason wasn't going to make it.

He'd had an aneurism, and he wasn't going to survive it.

Within the hour, I was again making the six-hour drive. I arrived at around midnight and he seemed calm. He seemed peaceful. When I grabbed his hand, he didn't wince. He had no feeling whatsoever.

As our Mom left the room, I dropped to my knees beside his bed and wept as I held the back of his hand to my forehead.

Jim had not been given a full explanation of his son's situation and when he arrived at the hospital shortly after 3am, Beth looked at me and said…

"I can't do it. Ben honey, please tell him."

As I walked out of Jason's room Jim was walking up.

I don't remember what I said to him exactly, I just remember Jim and I standing in the middle of the intensive care unit embracing each other as I whispered into his ear.

*Jesus wept.*
*John 11:35*
*KJV*

The very next day, I watched the monitor reveal the inevitable as pulse and blood pressure slowly descended.

I ran my fingers through his hair and told him good-bye.

I kissed his forehead and gripped him more tightly than I had anyone my entire life.

"I love you Jason. "

His heart beat its last, and I stood watching over him.

I couldn't do anything to help him.

My beloved Jason died.

*Every time I say your name in prayer—which is practically all the*
*time—I thank God for you, the God I worship with my whole life in the*
*tradition of my ancestors. I miss you a lot, especially when I remember*
*that last tearful good-bye, and I look forward to a joy-packed reunion.*
*2 Timothy 1:3-4*
*The Message*

# Friends

*When I was a Corrections* Officer, I hated my job.

When I awoke to get ready for work, I felt horrible knowing I had to get ready and go to a job I despised.

One morning, February 05, 2003 to be exact, I was leaving work and I decided I was through.

I was standing at the gate, waiting for it to unlock, and I somehow knew I would never be back.

Leading up to this point, I had felt trapped. I would look around and see officers who had been on the prison compound for 15, 20, or 25 years and they were all over-weight, unhealthy, and had extremely negative attitudes.

Putting up with inmates was the easy part. Don't get me wrong, having to fight a grown man covered in his own feces can get a little weird, and maybe a little stressful.

Or listening to an inmate tell you he shouldn't be in prison because the prosecuting attorney used the term stab when he really slashed his victim 63 times.

"I'm to be released because of a mistrial any day now" they would say.

Inmates had a way of viewing their situation much better than it actually was. What else could they do? We all knew they were full of it, but the disturbing part was that they were genuinely upset over the fact that they were only in prison because they felt like the prosecuting attorney cheated, not because they did something wrong.

I recall another conversation.

"She was begging me to 'give it to her', and I'm the one who gets in trouble." says a pervert serving 30 years.

"Who?" I ask regretfully.

"My niece. Everyone thinks because she's nine she can't be a manipulatin' bitch but I'm here to tell you…"

I know where this conversation is going and he's already starting to piss me off so I interrupt him.

"Get the hell away from me… now." End of conversation.

I expected to be repulsed from inmates, but not all were repulsive though.

I never expected it from the officers.

I had been going to the Law Enforcement Academy Monday through Friday from 6 p.m. to 10 p.m, and on Saturday from 8 a.m. to 5 p.m. During the week, I would leave the college, get home by 10:30 p.m, get ready for work, and leave by 11:15p.m. I worked from midnight to eight in the morning. I would sleep for a couple of hours, wake up, study, spend time with the wife and kids, and then head off to school again. After almost four months of keeping that schedule, I was tired. Tired of work. Tired of school. Tired of inmates. Tired of putting up with other people's junk.

So this particular morning in February, I had finally had enough. I worked extremely hard to be the best on the compound, only to be chastised by my lieutenant for trying to be the best. He cursed me for volunteering to do the things no one else wanted to do. He cursed me for doing my job faster and better than my peers most of the time.

He cursed me for being skinny. He cursed me for being in the Army Reserve and having to take a weekend off each month for training. He didn't like me.

That morning, I realized that it wasn't just him. I was unhappy. I felt disgusted with myself knowing I had no choice but to go to a place I hated five days a week. That's when it hit me. I was standing at the gate, waiting for someone to unlock it and it hit me. I didn't have to do this. I had recently been entertaining leaving and finally accepting repeated offers from my father to join him and my brother in the insurance industry. I ended up at that moment, in that place because of God's perfect purpose. This time, I can't selfishly proclaim his motive was solely for my educational experience.

A few months back, I had been placed under the supervision of a fifty year-old black woman named Marie. Marie was a Sergeant, and the kind of person that if she didn't like you, you'd be better off staying out of her way. Most officers on the compound stayed out of her way whether or not they knew if she did or didn't like them. She had been with the department of Corrections for more than twenty years, and was not apt to putting up with the likes of me. About the only thing you ever heard about Marie was that she was mean, rude, and racist.

All she knew of me was that I was an arrogant, G.I. Joe, Mr. Hard-charger who was a rude, pretentious prick. Looking back, I don't think her first impression was too far off-base.

Some say I was placed with her to either drive her to retirement or make me quit.

My first night with her, I was trying to do everything by the book, and the moment I didn't, Marie pointed it out.

I said "shit", and she snapped, "what did I tell you about that cussin'?"

"Sorry."

The first two weeks were a little rough. For both of us. She would press me as hard as she could because she could, and I would do little things just to piss her off. Most of a Corrections Officer's nights are spent in conversation with the other officer you are posted with. Not us. One could probably not compose a sentence with the number of cordial words she and I said to each other during the first two weeks..

Eight hours of silence.

Doing nothing.

Count inmates twice an hour and then…

Sit.

Then one night, Marie was visited by another Sergeant whom she liked. They spoke of different things, and in between listening to them, I counted inmates. When the other Sergeant left the dorm, I decided to try and leave off where their conversation ended. It had to do with a poem.

After about five minutes of silence, and beating myself up over whether or not I should try to start a conversation with her, I did it.

"*The Funeral*", I said.

"Do what?" she asked.

"*The Funeral*, by Gordon Parks. It's my favorite."

"You know a poem by Gordon Parks?" Her tone was very sarcastic and disbelieving.

"Sure. I chose to write an entire piece on that poem, and Gordon Parks, when I was in High School."

"Really?"

She and I began having a conversation.

She and I were still very unsure of each other, and neither of us was willing to throw any amount of trust into the other, but we began having a conversation.

The next night, when we returned to work, she had read the poem.

For the next few weeks we continued to speak to each other. Whatever we discussed, it seemed we debated and argued what we thought were our different viewpoints.

It was rough. Before, we didn't speak to each other because we didn't want anything to do with each other. Now it felt like we didn't want to speak to each other because we knew before the conversation began that we were not going to like what the other had to say. So instead of doing the mature thing and bypassing any conversation all together, we provoked one another incessantly.

The dim-witted person that each of us thought we were posted with, turned out to be a little more than we expected. I was a pompous ass. I didn't think this woman had a chance arguing with me about anything, especially politics. "Who is she to pretend I don't know what I'm talking about," I thought.

She was thinking, "who in the hell does he think he is, at half my age, telling me how things are?"

So after the two most hard-headed people on the compound battled for eight hours a day, five days a week, for about three months solid, something changed.

We realized our viewpoints were not much different. We realized we were very much the same. We enjoyed much of the same music. We enjoyed the same books and movies. We began to accept that we could educate each other.

I stopped talking, and listened to what this woman had to say.

I listened to her journey.

I soaked up her wisdom and became inquisitive. I looked forward to coming in to work because of her. Not that she really needed it, but I became protective of her. I learned she was a woman with many scars. She was incredibly strong. She was incredibly loving. She was intriguing.

I became genuinely interested in her life.

And do you know what? That's exactly what she needed.

We became like best friends.

She was appalled when she learned I had never seen *The Godfather*. So she brought in the entire series for me to take home and watch.

She started cooking for me. Never in twenty years of working in corrections did this woman regularly bring in food for anyone.

She was bringing me entire meals. While I took care of business, she was heating up food in the Officer's station microwave and preparing me a plate.

When my brother died, she was the only person on the planet to give me a card. Cards don't really heal a thing. A person who gives a card is the healing agent.

I think we both were healing agents to each other.

She became very fond of my wife and children.

We genuinely cared for each other.

Her youngest son was in prison, and her eldest son only spoke to her when he needed something from her.

No matter what, no matter how hard this woman became, she was still a sensitive, caring mother. She loved her 'boys', and I'm sure they loved her as well. Once a month, she would go and visit her son in a prison about 60 miles away. She had to conduct her visits on non-prison visitation times due to the fact that she was a corrections officer and being recognized by inmates on another compound could put her son in danger. So every month, she visited him, by herself, and put money into his account. She was hard on him, but he had no one else. His mother was the only one. Marie continuously tried to get her oldest son to visit his brother but to no avail.

Even if you do something so horribly wrong you get sent to prison, mom will still love you.

Hmmm.

Interesting relationship.

Whenever I wonder if I'm able to love the way Jesus wants me to love, I think about Marie. I think about my mother and my father.

What could she possibly benefit from keeping up a relationship with her son while he's in prison? It's not like he's going anywhere. Why spend time and money on someone you get nothing out of? Honestly. What could someone in prison possibly provide someone on the outside?

There is a shred of hope for me. If it were my kids, I would love them the same way. So, I am able to love the way Jesus wants me to love. Unconditionally. Unending. I am only able to do this because of Him, and he is the ultimate example. But somehow, through Marie's example and how extensively complicated her situation was, and my relationship with Christ and my relationship with my children, I see, I can love exactly the way he wants me to.

No more excuses. Think about it.

So I was in the middle of experiencing a valuable lesson I wouldn't actually learn until years later.

However, it wasn't going to end as poetic as that. Everything was going great, until my Lieutenant started in on me. Marie would stick up for me, and it was well known I was not to be fooled with lest you deal with her wrath, but to our Lieutenant, it didn't matter. He didn't like Marie, and he hated me.

He actually asked me one day if I was willing to be on his "team".

"You see, I have a 'corps' of people who I like being around me here." He arrogantly articulated as He gripped both of his hands together tightly as if to illustrate an imaginary nucleus of correctional officer personnel bound together by the unbreakable bond of loyalty. "This 'corps' of people takes care of me and I, in turn, take care of them. Do you understand what I'm trying to tell you?"

My response ensured I would not be with the Department of Corrections much longer.

"Well, yes-sir I do. I understand completely. But what I don't understand, is why the hell you're telling me this."

Not smart. I knew he would scream before he uttered a word. Veins protruded from atop his bald head as it became increasingly more red. I was told to leave, very colorfully, and that I wouldn't last under his watch. As I walked out of his office, he said, "I will end you on this compound. Your fuckin' days are numbered smart-ass."

Turns out, the bastard was right.

So here I am, standing with Marie a few days later at the gate. February 5th, 2003.

"I think I'm done Marie."

She looked at me with a surprised look… "Do what?"

"I think I'm done," I say again.

"You're serious aren't you baby?"

"Yes ma'am, I think I am."

Marie told me to call her later and let me know if I was coming in tonight or not.

I felt like the most powerful man in the world. No one, nothing could stop me. I had the power over the lieutenant who hated me. I controlled my own destiny. I was in charge of my life. Rest on this for a second. Do you know how liberating it is to say "I quit." This was the first time I had done this. Ever. I was free. No more midnight shifts. No more working on weekends, no more working on the holidays. I would now make my own schedule. I would be my own boss. If I didn't feel like going to work I wouldn't.

I'm going to spend more time with the kids.

My wife will be happy. She never slept in the bed without me. Five nights a week she slept on the couch.

She'll never sleep on the couch again.

I drove home thinking about me. A completely Godless inner monologue about me and who *I am*. My relationship with Christ was nothing more than an irreverent, disrespectful passing quip whenever a situation necessitated.

My problem with this whole 'God Thing', was that I was unaware I could actually have a relationship that mattered. I worked hard; I was an over-achiever at most things, and an under-achiever at others. I was different from other people because I knew I could do what-ever I wanted to do, accomplish what I wanted to accomplish. In the Marine Corps we would say that we had the ability to negotiate any obstacle. Adapt and overcome. My personality embodied that philosophy. Personal power. Don't let your mind get in the way.

"Mind over matter. If you don't mind, it don't matter."

So it was still all about me. What I can do for my family. What I can do for my life. I had no idea of God's role in every aspect of not only that day, but every moment leading up to that point in time. I smiled like a giddy little school girl for the entire twenty-two minute trip it took me to get home. I just knew I had made the right decision to leave. The wrong decision couldn't feel this good. I was trying to imagine what it would be like to finally be accountable for my own work ethic. I always worked harder than everyone else, so I believed in my inevitable success in sales. I decided this is going to be the biggest announcement in my family. This is great news.

I walked into my house, ready to proudly proclaim to my wife how our lives are now going to be better. After all, I worked forty hours a week at a job I hated that demanded an odd set of work hours. It was difficult for my wife and kids to adapt to my schedule. And for what? Nothing more rewarding than a less than average income?

My children were eating breakfast, and my wife was in the shower. I sat on the bathroom counter and told her, "I'm done."

"Done with what?"

"I'm finished with the prison. I quit."

We talked about everything that was wrong with my job, and talked about everything that was right with the new career I had selected. We talked about everything that was wrong in our life and attributed it to my job, and how everything would be made right with the new one.

I met with my father at his office and told him my plans. He had been waiting for years to hear me say I was coming to work with him. We both agreed it was the best decision for me and my family, and we were to begin the transition right away. I told him I would meet him for lunch and we would talk about it more but I had to stop by my Army Reserve Unit to let them know I wouldn't be participating in

65

our field training exercise that weekend. The "FTX" as we called it, was a three day excursion into the forest to practice Military Police combat and combat support tactics. I figured I had enough going on and I didn't need to complicate the situation more by leaving for three days to run off into the woods and play G.I. Joe.

My wife, my father, and everyone else in my family felt great about what I was going to do.

Everything would be just fine.

From here on out...

Life was gonna be great.

*Romans 1:28*
*Since they didn't bother to acknowledge God, God quit bothering them and let them run loose. And then all hell broke loose...*

# See you in a year

*. . . I pulled* into the parking lot of the 351ˢᵗ MP Company at around 11:00 am on Wednesday, February 5ᵗʰ, 2003. As I pulled in I wondered why there were around forty cars in the parking lot on a Wednesday. Forty cars or so is usually indicative of a Saturday or Sunday during a drill weekend. The middle of the week seemed a little odd, and no matter how euphoric a state I was in, I could not help but take notice of it.

A friend of mine was walking across the parking lot so I sped up as if to imply I were going to run him over.

I pulled up to him and laughed.

"What are you doing?" I asked.

"I came up here to figure out what was going on."

"What are you talking about?" I ask, very confused.

"You didn't get a phone call?

"No,.. what are you talking about?"

"Why are you here?" He asked.

"I came to let them know I won't be here this weekend."

"You're serious?" He's almost grimacing in pain but he wants to laugh.

"Stop screwing around, what's up?" Now I want to know.

"We are getting deployed."

It's funny how our minds play a picture show of future episodes of our life in which we handle everything in coolest, most professional manner. Of course I didn't see this coming, nor did I handle it as cool as I always thought I would.

An hour later, I sat down with my family for lunch at a restaurant we frequented. I told them I was being deployed for an operation and I didn't know when or where I was going, and I didn't know for how long.

My whole life seemed to come down to this.

As a child, nearly every young man plays "Army". Except for the boy with an unusually advanced stage of arrogance who declares he's playing "Marine". I did it, my brother did it, and all of our friends did it. Almost everyone can remember, the countless hours hiding in plain site believing no one can see you; the constant rolling of the tongue in an attempt to perfect the sound of a machine-gun with your mouth. Yep, there was no superpower me, a couple of buddies, and an array of plastic look-alike weaponry couldn't conquer. I remember arguing with my friends all day long about how rank structure was made up, and the correct way military time was told. "I got you, I got you" we'd scream actually believing we riddled our opponents body with imaginary bullets. Sometimes we'd scream, "That's not fair!"

That's not fair.

Our enemies usually rotated between the Russian's and G.I. Joe's Nemesis, Cobra. We threw the word "commie" around like we had a clue what it meant or why it was bad. No one ever showed up to play and said, "let's overthrow a tyrannous, maniacal dictator in the Middle East and liberate generations of human beings born under oppressive rule."

War was so glamorous.

Too glamorous.

I was always on the lookout for walkie-talkie radios, m-16's, grenades, and pistols which possessed the most life-like appearance. Acceptable, appropriate war time attire began with one of my Dad's old army jackets and grew to necessitate camouflage trousers and blouse and inevitably, face paint. Tree branches stuffed in every pocket, tear, buttonhole or belt-loop was attributed to looks rather than any functional purpose concerning basic combat tactics of breaking up the body's silhouette.

John Rambo. The best warrior-soldier of all. I need to be like him. But I can't forget, Arnold slaughters an entire island of bad-guys in Commando, so I'll be him too. I need to fight like them. I need to be them. John Rambo and Commando have never been beaten up. My emulation of the two at this young age set a pattern of escapism I believe I'm plagued with to this very day. What would Rambo do? How would he respond? How would he train? I can be like him.

How appealing that is to a child who has been beaten up a few hundred times. Maybe this is what it came down to. No one ever becomes John Rambo. Killing isn't that easy, and not getting killed isn't that easy. But to attain the closest level of bad-ass to Rambo warrants many ass-whippings. I had my ass kicked so many times I figured I was the guy who won't grow up to be able to do anything. I won't be tough. I won't be able to fight because it's just not in me to do so.

As God's purpose in my life emerged, it raised questions. Did God Create a fighter? Could God's diagrammatic illustration of my life have included plans for a fighter? Every person on the planet has the propensity for violence, but was my past prophetic, and did it provide the vehicle for my predilection for violence?

Deep down, I wanted to help people. Giving back and being the hero in someone's life was at the core of my desire. Hurting people and having the ability to cause pain seemed, for so many years, an added benefit.

My penchant for harming the harmful seemed to be a natural gift. So what does that say about my past?

As a parent, I decided not to allow my son to own fake guns. Funny thing is, I would be genuinely frustrated when he would pretend a tinker-toy was a pistol. Try as I may, I just can't stop him from playing the same games I played. Why should I?

For years I walked past my grandfather's award case and not once had I truly respected its contents. I thought I did, just like I thought I could whip four-hundred thousand Russians had I real guns. My grandfather was a humble man. I could claim his lack of desire for speaking about the two wars he served didn't help me much to understand his sacrifice. But one day, I heard my mother say to him: "Daddy, are you going to give Ben your medals one day?" He replied as any nurturing grandfather would. "Hell no, tell 'em to get his own." You see, he wanted to give them to his granddaughters. As he and my grandmother so subtly put it on occasions to numerous to count, "Women got no God-damn place on the battlefield." What a coach. I really did want the medals. I really wanted to earn my own. But there I was, young, patriotic, and without a clue. Naïveté.

All I wanted was to help people. I wanted a military career my entire childhood. As the first Gulf War erupted I remember thinking how badly I wish I could serve. Men from our church, as well as my 9th grade Geography teacher were unexpectedly pulled from their lives to fulfill their commitment, and it seemed to hurt my soul badly. I was fourteen, and I hated every minute of it because I couldn't be there. I was proud of my country, proud of the brave men and women who served, and pissed off because I wasn't old enough to fight. Naïveté.

So I trained. Everything to me was training. In high-school I joined the Navy Junior Reserve Officer Training Corps, known as R.O.T.C. How well I performed in everything I did throughout my R.O.T.C. career somehow seemed to indicate the level of greatness I would attain when I joined the military. My body had not yet matured so I was disadvantaged athletically. I worked harder. I checked out a rifle to practice my rifle drill at home when no one else did. I ran farther than the farthest runner. I spit-shined, Ironed, polished and creased more than the highest ranking seniors. I learned to conduct drill. I learned to call commands. I listened to the best of the best critique the best, and learned from it. All because I believed this would make me a better warrior.

Years later, I realize that mindset is policy in the United States Military. Too bad it really doesn't mean shit.

So here I was at lunch with my family.

I'm actually slated to go to war.

The war hasn't started yet, but I'm secretly praying it will. The activation and deployment of my Army Reserve MP unit is an auspicious sign that War is imminent.

Aside from leaving my wife and kids for six months and the threat of being killed, going to war is a long awaited wonderful prospect. I wanted to get on the bus with gun in hand and get to killin' before someone changed their mind.

To hell with these people I thought. I've been taking garbage off of people my whole life. I've been beaten up and abused repeatedly. It's time for me to bring it back to those who are doing it to others.

I tell my family it will be hard to leave them.

It's time for me to do my part as an American Patriot and put my life endanger to protect innocent lives and preserve the American way.

I tell my three year-old daughter and my four year-old son I'm leaving to fight the bad-guys. I tell them Daddy has to accept responsibility because no one else will.

I'm really thinking about when I was fourteen and my discontent for watching the Gulf War against Saddam Hussein on television and how excited I am now that I am on the brink of an opportunity to fight him and his genocidal regime.

I assure my mother and father along with my wife that I'll not try to be a hero and get myself killed.

I'm really hoping for a glorious fight in which I distinguish myself in battle.

I remind my family that I have been training for this my entire life.

I wonder if I'm ready, and for a brief moment I realize that the most skilled and ferocious warrior can do nothing to protect himself when mortar and rocket attacks occur and befall victims by mere chance.

I have hoped for war longer than I can remember.

The next two weeks were filled with packing, re-packing, inventory, re-packing, re-inventory, and re-packing equipment used by my same MP unit in the first Gulf War. During that time, my nights at home were very consciously spent with my wife and children. Every moment seemed sacred. Every time we laughed I thought of where I was going and the imminent danger I would inevitably face.

Every moment I spent with them was one less moment I had.

I loaded up at the bookstore, choosing literature I never took the time to read. I started out with *The Grapes of Wrath*, *Dante's Inferno*, *Tortilla Flat*, and *The Count of Monte Cristo*. Two weeks after arriving at Ft. Stewart, I had finished them and was ready to move on to more Steinbeck. I bought and read *Cannery Row*, and re-read *Of Mice and Men*. I read *Memnoch the Devil*, by Anne Rice, *Education of a Wandering Man* by Louis La'mour, and a few political commentary books along the way. Although The Grapes of Wrath and The Count of Monte Cristo were arguably two of the better pieces of literature ever produced, it was another I read that caused a stir among my fellow soldiers.

Mein Kampf.

I was curious.

I wondered how a man, a formerly jailed political activist, made a somewhat lower developed country into a world superpower in only a decade. I wondered, behind what logic and reason could a person preach such hatred for an entire race of people and desire to punish them with torture and murder? After all, wasn't Saddam Hussein guilty of genocidally murdering the Kurds as blatantly did Hitler the Jews? Could I somehow figure out what goes on in the mind of a terrorist hell-bent on killing those who don't share racial and ethnic backgrounds and religious ideologies? I thought so. However, my fellow soldiers didn't. They didn't want to? Part of the problem was when you see a near six-foot tall blonde-haired blue-eyed man reading the so-called Nazi bible, it screams stereotype. I knew that and I thought it was funny. What added to my delight in the irony of the situation was that a couple of weeks before I even thought about reading that ridiculous book, I, like many other male soldiers headed to a hundred and fifty degree, dust covered combat zone, shaved my head completely bald for hygienic reasons.

When asked why I was reading such a book by three of my closest friends, I always responded with a very true and accurate answer. One that resembles what I wrote above. As people walked by my bunk and observed my choice of reading material they often asked..

"Why are you reading that shit?"

I would respond, "To try and understand how an entire nation grips religious fanaticism and stands behind the murder of innocent life because of a perverted interpretation of God."

"Seriously, why are you reading that shit?" The question always repeated. Not one time did someone take the true and accurate answer. Never. So my response the second time around?

"Because I'm a racist redneck white trash piece of shit who desperately needs an identity to cling to in this ever-changing world of diversity."

"I'm trying to be serious."

"I am too," I say with a smile.

"No you're not. I just wanted to know why you would read such thing…"

"And I answered you. But my answer wasn't what you wanted to hear so I gave you the answer you were really looking for."

I found out years later that my rants about why I was reading Mein Kampf actually resonated with some of my fellow soldiers and they ended up using that perspective to give speeches and write papers for school.

Ft. Stewart.

As I stood in the middle of our squad-bay holding my bags in my hands, I remember telling myself that our living conditions are going to enable us to toughen up.

Yeah…okay.

The walls were cinder-block, and the floor was cement. The roof was made of wood slats, meagerly covered with shingles. There was no heat, no air-conditioning, and no bathroom. The bay held around twenty old military-style, steel bunk-beds on each side. The mattresses smelled like mildew and most looked like a used diaper or butcher's apron.

The bathrooms were located in a separate building adjacent to our barracks. Same construction as the squad-bay, but with showers and toilets. In fact, in the middle of the room, stood a three feet high, eight-inch thick divider wall that had five toilets on one side, and five on the other. The toilets, from one to the next, side to side were no more than 24 inches apart, and had nothing in between them. This makes a situation incredibly awkward when two grown men are sitting on a latrine taking care of their business and their knees keep bumping. However, we did grow strangely comfortable with holding a serious conversation while sitting there. To complicate the bathroom experience further, soldiers sitting on toilets on one side of the wall were mere inches away from the backsides of soldiers standing at the sinks; soldiers sitting on toilets on the other side of the wall were facing the back-sides of those using urinals.

The showers were unbelievably atrocious. The walls seemed to be thirty different colors due to the years of painting over the older, peeling, mildewed coats. Black mildew and green algae enhanced the shockingly vile condition of the walls, especially below each of the rusted, calcium deposited shower heads which originated from the same hole in the cinder block walls that the roaches seemed to enjoy running to and from. A putrid smell arose from the drain and became increasingly worse when hot water was applied. The concrete floor was littered with used band -aids which at some point covered the sores on soldier's arms caused by the small-pox vaccine.

This is how we lived for three months. Originally we were only supposed to be at Ft Stewart for a couple of weeks. A couple of weeks turned into a month. A month turned into two, and two into three.

The first couple of weeks at Ft. Stewart were pretty busy. During the day we trained, exercised, unpacked and re-packed equipment, and held formations. In the evening, we drank beer, listened to music, or read books. That is until alcohol was banned briefly because of a drunken brawl in front of my barracks.

My wife and children would make the four hour drive on Fridays, and we would all stay in a hotel room for the weekend. I missed my wife and children more than I ever thought I could. Every time they dropped me off at my barracks to head home, I felt sick.

Each week, this continued.

I, along with the rest of the unit, started to think we weren't going. It worried me. I was actually afraid I would have to go back home and face my family after getting deployed for war, and not have gone.

I trained; day in, day out, and wondered if I was really going to go. Wars were for the history books and I just couldn't picture myself having played a part.

To me, it was like daydreaming about winning the lottery. It would be great; it is just too good to be true.

After three months at Ft Stewart, we finally got a flight to Kuwait.

The day we flew to Kuwait, a crowd of soldiers gathered to pray and sing old hymns behind the barracks. For the first time since this deployment began, I participated in a public prayer. I felt out of place but I felt like there was no other place I wanted to be.

When we arrived in Kuwait, it was around midnight, and nearly 100 degrees. We entered a large tent for a briefing, and afterwards, we made our way to a tent assigned to our entire Company. Somewhere around 170 soldiers piled into a tent, and we quickly realized that all of our gear would have to be stored outside. At this point, any attempt to lay down and sleep was pointless for me. I was too excited. I was actually in Kuwait. I wandered around the base camp for a couple of hours and just before 4 a.m, I noticed the horizon began to appear increasingly brighter. I couldn't for the life of me understand what the light was until an hour later when it was obvious it was the sun.

The temperature began to rise in the driest climate I have ever been. As the sun pounded the sand, the heat radiated upward. The wind picked it up, and the result resembled the opening of an oven door and having your breath taken away.

Just walking across our base camp sucked.

We ended up running missions for almost three months in Kuwait before we moved into Iraq. Before the move, my team was selected to run security missions for supply routes from the Kuwait border, to a small base about a hundred and fifty miles into Iraq.

War no longer seemed exciting.

It was not as glorious as I had imagined.

"Hours of sheer boredom punctuated by moments of sheer terror."

Someone once said that about something not of war.

I find it to be an acutely accurate description.

One day, in the early weeks of our tour, my team was called for a mission into Basrah, the second largest city in Iraq. As we loaded up our humvee, we were put on standby.

Evidently, the tactical operations center didn't think it would be a good idea to send troops through the massive rioting that had broken out. The tribal leaders in Basrah were withholding fuel, water, and electricity from the good people of Basrah, and they weren't happy.

After hours of waiting, all missions for the day were cancelled. The next morning however, we were first up for pulling a mission.

We were to escort three trucks to a small Coalition Forces Base situated in the heart of Basrah.

The first truck was a tanker truck carrying 32,000 liters of gas.

The second was a flat-bed tractor trailer loaded to the top with bottled water.

The third, was a pickup truck driven by a civilian contractor who, after arriving at our destination, got out of his truck, threw his Kevlar helmet and stated…

"Fuck this. I fucking quit. I'm going the fuck home."

I'll admit. The ride in was a little unpleasant.

That was when I started feeling like I needed God.

I really started praying.

How funny.

For the next eleven months, I continued to pray. I gave no consideration to actually having a relationship with Jesus Christ, but I prayed. There may not have been a night I went to sleep without praying. If there was, it was few and far between. I had a feeling that if I didn't pray, something bad was going to happen. The most important thing I had to pray for was my wife and children. I would make myself sick worrying about them. So I prayed for their safety. I prayed for my safety. Not because I was consumed with a personal fear of dying, but because I feared my wife and children's world being turned upside down had something happened to me. So I actually believed that God could somehow hear me. I believed that by praying to God, I could actually influence the outcome of a situation that has the propensity to be bad. Somewhere inside I believed that God was powerful enough to change my life from every facet imaginable. So with this belief in mind, coupled with a gripping fear that consumes most of my thoughts as I lie awake wondering what horrible thing Is happening right now to my wife and my children, and thinking about the mortars that just about landed on my head while sitting back on my cot inside my tent, I think or believe, that just maybe, God can make my life all better. Funny, that of all the things he has on his mind, all the things he has to do and take care of, all the complaining and whining going on about him across the planet, he is in the middle of a war that I am fighting, and I think that he cares about me enough to care about how uncomfortable I am with this war, and with myself.

Yet I still saw no need to worship HIM.

I treated him no differently that someone who is nice to another because they can get something out of it. Deep down, I knew he could help. I knew he had the power to save me, and I refused to worship.

I actually made a conscious decision to not truly believe in his power.

It wasn't until after I returned to my family from the war, did I start believing.

When I got back home, my world was turned upside down. Everything I thought I knew before the war, changed.

I had changed.

My family had changed.

God brought me to my knees and it was only then, did I realize...I needed HIM.

My life would be incomplete without HIM.

I tried a new job.

It didn't work.

I tried counseling.

That didn't work either.

Once again, I felt alone.

For nearly seventeen months, my life revolved around a base camp. I ate four times a day. I lifted weights and took my supplements on a very strict schedule. I listened to music, read books, and smoked more cigarettes than I can count.

I didn't have to worry about bills. I didn't have to worry about the kids getting to and from school. I didn't have to worry about mowing the lawn or taking out the trash. Laundry was a service provided to us so I didn't even have to worry about washing my clothes.

All I had to do was run missions. Sure, getting shot at was nerve-racking. Mortar's and I.E.D's were a little scary. But life was simple.

Back home, I found out that my family kept living. Life wasn't put on hold when I left for the war like I subconsciously thought it had. The gunfire that was nerve-racking and the I.E.D's that were a little scary began to haunt me. Those little things turned out to be big things.

The two soldier's in my unit who didn't return to their families began to weigh heavily on my mind.

All of the brutal images that I can never 'un-see' returned ruthlessly.

My wife and children sometimes wondered who came back from the war.

I wondered who came back too.

It seemed nothing made sense.

The more I realized I didn't have anything under control, the more I spun out of control.

And God, in his perfect timing stepped in.

God brought me to my knees and it was only then, did I realize... I needed HIM. I realized that my life would remain incomplete without HIM.

The only way God was going to reach me was by bringing me to my knees.

The only way I was going to find my way back to what God had planned for me, was to make me realize I wasn't at all as big as I thought I was.

There was only one way for me to begin to see what my whole life up to this point was about.

# Me and Jesus

*...For everyone to whom much is given,*
*from him much will be required.*
*Luke 12:48*
*NKJV*

*Jesus loves me.*

I was in the shower one day, thinking about all I've experienced in my past, and I started to think about things I wish I could change.

Then I started thinking about the consequences of those changes.

I didn't like them.

I started thinking maybe it was better to have lived through it.

It's over now.

Gone.

All that's left is the memory. As painful as the memory might be sometimes, I start thinking that just maybe, it's worth it.

I started to realize that everything that has happened to me, good or bad, has had a profound affect on my life, which inevitably led to who I am. The conclusion was that I like who I am. I like what I have become. I like knowing what I know. Sure there are things I wish I could "un-see", but those are the things which have enabled me to see this life that God has given me through a lens not often perceived. Then it hit me. Of all the times I've thought of blessings, I never thought of the dreadful, or the seemingly counter-productive-to-my-life as such.

Could it have all been planned?

Did I become what the world made me?

I thought of my creation, and I could almost see it:

Jesus is standing there before an undistinguishable shape and He's talking to it. He's re-assuring in his tone. He's saying; "I'm gonna make your body strong. You'll be resilient. You'll be able to withstand great physical demands and punishment. Your mind, I'll make stronger. I'll give you an high aptitude to think, interpret and remember what you experience and learn. You'll have the ability to withstand great pressure and the tasks I'm going to set before you. Your heart will be loving. My kind of love. More love than your mind can comprehend, which in turn will be too much for your body to feel. Your soul, like the rest of you, is mine. However, you will have the choice to do with it what you want. Your soul will be the foundation of all I have built in you. The gifts I am giving you and their power will be dependent upon what you decide with your soul. You will choose to be what the world wants you to be, or you will choose what I want you to be. This gift of choice, as well as all others, comes with a price. I'm going to allow you to experience complete joy, peace, and happiness, but I'm also going to allow you to experience desperation and hopelessness. You are going to live through things I won't allow others to live through. You will experience hardships I won't allow others to experience. It will be tough. You'll want to give up. Sometimes you will feel utterly lost, defenseless, weak, beaten, and confused to the highest degree. You will hurt. You will feel pain at levels higher than you can imagine survivable. Your gifts will seem to clash. But know, as I am here with you now, I will be with you always. Never forget; the dream that I have for you is in fact, mine. I designed you. I created you. And I have done so with perfect purpose. You, your goals, your life, your history, and your future…are mine.

*It's in Christ that we find out who we are and what we are living for.*
*Long before we first heard of Christ and got our hopes up, he had his eye*
*on us, had designs on us for glorious living, part of the overall purpose he*
*is working out in everything and everyone.*
*Ephesians 1:11*
*The Message*

There was a prophet named Jeremiah whom God tells "Before I formed you in the womb I knew you; Before you were born I sanctified you; I ordained you a prophet to the nations." (Jeremiah 1:5, NKJV) I would imagine Jesus' pre-birth talk with Jeremiah was similar in format to mine. God showed me that scripture about a year after I imagined Jesus' talk with me.

Just when I started thinking that maybe this scenario is nothing but a fantasy I have fabricated, Jesus sends me a message. A message that stings a little. He said he would be with me always. I guess I just needed to listen more closely.

There is a story in the Bible where Jesus tells his disciples that he wants to go across a lake. So they all pile into this boat and Jesus goes to sleep. Then a terrible storm arises and the waves violently crash against the ship and the disciples begin panicking.

Where's Jesus?

He's asleep.

On a pillow as attributed to one account.

That's funny.

Never did I imagine I question Jesus' motives like that. I read this story and pretentiously wondered how, after seeing Jesus perform miracle after miracle with their own eyes, could these men have allowed themselves to fear the storm?

Only when I go back to my idea of how I came into being and read the about the disciples reaction to the storm does the answer come to me.

Jesus owns the dream.

The messiah himself told them "Let *us* go to the other side…". He set their path before them.

He directed them where to go. He told them their destination. It was His idea. This important piece of information escapes the disciples. It escapes me. That is why we are afraid. I have forgotten that *my* life is His. Just as he told me; you, your goals, your life your history, and your future…are mine. He owns the dream. So when the storms arise, and I start acting like Jesus isn't paying attention, I am being as ridiculous as anyone who has ever doubted, if not more. And like the disciples, when Jesus wakes up, looks at me and says, "where is your faith?", I feel ridiculous. Jesus knew about the storm. In fact, the storm was the point for our little trip.

The storm is over, the sea is calm, and aside from being completely soaked and feeling a little ashamed, all is fine.

*Do what your king commands; you gave a sacred oath of obedience. Don't worryingly second-guess your orders or try to back out when the task is unpleasant. You're serving his pleasure, not yours. The king has the last word. Who dares say to him, "what are you doing?" Carrying out orders won't hurt you a bit; the wise person obeys promptly and accurately. Yes, there's a right time and way for everything, even though, unfortunately, we miss it for the most part.*
*Ecclesiastes 8:2-7*

# What He Didn't Say...

*" follow me."*
*John 21:19*
*NKJV*

*" feed my lambs."*
*John 21:15*
*NIV*

*" feed my sheep."*
*John 21:16*
*NIV*

*"Go into the world.*
*Go everywhere and announce the Message*
*of God's good news to one and all."*
*Mark 16:15*
*The Message*
*NKJV*

*"You shall love the LORD your God*
*with all your heart,*
*with all your soul, and*
*with all your mind."*
*Matthew 22:37*
*NKJV*

*"But I say to you who hear:*
*Love your enemies,*
*do good to those who hate you..."*
*Luke 6:27*
*NKJV*

*"You shall love the LORD your God*
*with all your heart,*
*with all your soul,*
*with all your strength, and*
*with all your mind,' and '*
*your neighbor as yourself."*
*Luke 10:27*
*NKJV*

*"For God so loved the world*
*that He gave His only begotten Son,*
*that whoever believes in Him*
*should not perish but have everlasting life."*
*John 3:16*
*NKJV*

*"A new commandment I give to you,*
*that you love one another;*
*as I have loved you,*
*that you also love one another."*
*John 13:34*
*NKJV*

*"This is My commandment, that you love one another as I have loved you."*
*John 15:12*
*NKJV*

*"These things I command you, that you love each other."*
*John 15:17*
*NIV*

*"Peace I leave with you,*
*My peace I give to you;*
*not as the world gives*
*do I give to you.*
*Let not your heart be troubled,*
*neither let it be afraid."*
*John 14:27*
*NKJV*

*"These things I have spoken to you,*
*that in Me you may have peace.*
*In the world you will have tribulation;*
*but be of good cheer, I have overcome the world."*
*John 16:33*
*NKJV*

So Jesus is walking along the Sea of Galilee soon after he begins his ministry. He sees two brothers, Simon and Andrew who are fisherman.

What does he say?

Think about this. This is one of the most important things Jesus ever said.

He's the Messiah.

He was sent by God.

He *is* God.

He is a man.

He is setting out on the most profound journey in the history of mankind.

This is the beginning of the most important journey ever.

He is going to be saving people's souls.

He will teach people how to live and survive the cruelty of this world.

He is the King of Kings!

And two fishermen are the first people he talks to.

Fisherman.

I grew up fishing, recreationally. After a long day of fishing, I smell. I'm dirty. I don't look like much either. I look like a red-neck. People probably don't put much stock in me when they see a dirty redneck in a filthy white t-shirt and jeans that needs to shave.

That is after one day of fishing.

This guy Simon and his brother Andrew are fisherman. They do it day in, day out. Of course, the hygiene standards of a couple thousand years ago were probably no where near the standard we have set at current day so, I'm gonna go out on a limb and say they were nasty.

Here's the King of the Universe, walking along the water, and he stops and talks to two fisherman.

Imagine what the conversation must have looked like.

Jesus must have told the Simon and Andrew that he was going to preach the word of God and he wanted to recruit them. He must have told them that to get on board with this new ministry program they would first have to change a few things.

"You're going to have to clean yourselves up. You need to get some decent clothing that is clean, doesn't smell like fish, and doesn't have holes in it. I need you to look presentable. Clean and trim your fingernails. I'm sure with a little hard work you can get all of the old fish-guts and grime out. You need to trim your beards and get a haircut. Also, you need to clean up your language. You cuss like… well…sailors and you need to stop. Work on your grammar. If you're going to be speaking with me, for me, about me, and helping me spread the most important message on earth, you are going to have to do it with a little class. It's time to start acting like professionals. You need to look professional, and you need to sound professional. It's the whole package. I can't have you represent me and not look and be your best."

That is not what Jesus said.

Jesus walked up to these two brothers and simply said…

"Follow me."

Jesus didn't tell them how everything was going to be.

Jesus didn't tell them that everything would be great and how much peace they would have in their life.

Jesus didn't tell them that everything was going to get really strange.

Jesus didn't tell them that their life was now going to be increasingly complicated.

Jesus didn't tell them that they were going to endure some serious pain because of him.

Jesus didn't tell them that they were going to experience immense joy because of him.

Jesus told them…

"Follow me."

How hard is that for me to accept? Well, the Bible says it, so it must be true. Yet I still find myself wanting to talk to people about Jesus, and I want to tell them all the things Jesus didn't say. I want to create the perfect sales pitch…

Build rapport. Address the problem. Scare them. Sell the Solution. Relieve them. Address all rebuttals before the speech ends. Bring them to the point where they don't know how they got this far without your product, and they don't know what they'll do if they don't sign up, right now.

Jesus did not take that approach.

He didn't take that approach with Simon and Andrew, nor did he take it with two other fishermen who were brothers, James and John. He didn't even take that approach when he ran into Matthew.

Now there's an interesting Jesus encounter.

Matthew was a tax-collector. In Bible times this was bad. In today's world, Matthew wouldn't be everyone's poster child for the IRS; he would be a gangster. He stole money. He skimmed off of the top. He kicked people when they were down and he got rich off of it. Imagine a Mafioso used-car salesman with a couple of pipe-hitters coming to collect money you owe them.

What does Jesus say to him?

"Follow me."

Why?

Why does Jesus tell these men to follow him? Why doesn't he tell them to change? Simon, Andrew, James and John really had nothing to go on but a man standing before them telling them that he will make them fishers of men. It had to happen just that way. Matthew was able to see a few of Jesus' works. Matthew probably heard the rumors that the Messiah had come. He had probably also heard that Jesus was nothing but a fluke. When Jesus came to him and told him "follow me", Matthew went. It had to happen that way.

Jesus seemingly came out of nowhere, and told guys who were near the bottom of the social totem pole to simply follow him. They did. He didn't tell them that they were to change everything they were before they decided to come with him. Jesus knew that by these men spending time with him, they would change from the inside out. They would become more like God's idea of who they were created to be.

That's it.

Matthew shows us that we have all been subject to the miracles of Jesus Christ, and we have all been subject to the religious talk. We've all heard what everyone has to say about Jesus, yet maybe we have refused to see what he has to say about himself. For a long time I lived on a diet of my pastor's delivery of God's word. I later learned that if I were to live on a diet of God's written word, God would speak to me. If only I would read, and listen.

I started teaching an adult Sunday school class and when I had to teach, I studied. I studied hard. I felt like maybe I wasn't ready to be teaching people about the Bible. God must have thought differently. While studying and preparing for the lessons, I started hearing God more clearly than ever before. God started showing me what he wanted, and how he wanted me to do it. The more I read, and soaked up His Word, the more I wanted it. When I started teaching eleventh graders, I started teaching more on what the Bible had to say about what was going on in their lives. I became involved. I immersed myself in the Bible, focused on getting closer to God, and praying that he would show me the way to change my students' lives. And God did just that. He was changing me in the process. God started showing me how to take an undiluted message and deliver it to teenage boys who are walking right through the middle of a world of insanity.

I started seeing what Jesus said.

I started seeing what Jesus didn't say.

Why did I start seeing what He didn't say? Because I saw what Jesus said, and started seeing how backwards we often get his message.

I was talking with a friend one night who is divorced, has two boys that he gets on the weekend, and lives by himself. He told me that he wished he could be a man of God like me but he just can't. So I invite him to church because he told me that I understood him because he believes in God. His response?

"I don't know if I'm ready to. There's just some things I'm not willing to give up."

"Really? Like what?" I ask.

"Like women. I love to be with women…and I like porn. I don't want to give that up right now. I've got too much going on to worry about giving that stuff up."

Interesting huh? Here is a guy who I know is struggling with his faith in God and wants to have a personal relationship with Christ and doesn't have the first clue as to how to do it. Somehow he believes that he is supposed to be something he isn't before he goes to church. He thinks he is supposed to change who he is, and become a better person before he is saved.

So I reply, "So don't give it up right now."

I get a look. A look forever burned in my mind. So I continue…

"No one is asking you to give up that stuff right now. I'm inviting you to church. I am challenging you to not give that stuff up. I'm asking you to consider a relationship with Jesus Christ. Start there. Stop worrying about all the shit you have to stop doing. All I ask is that you have a conversation with our Father. Talk to him."

This guy's idea of Jesus' message is backwards. Jesus said, "follow me." What he didn't say was give up all the bad stuff, then follow me.

When we decide to follow Jesus, and truly accept that only he can save us, something changes inside us. All of the stuff I used to worry about having to give up…I don't do any more. Not just because it doesn't fit with America's idea of a good Christian. Not only because the Bible explicitly tells us there are certain things we must not do, but because I don't want to do them anymore. I don't care about them anymore. I find far more joy being picked on by eight year-old girls while teaching them basketball than getting drunk.

*So here's what I want you to do, God helping you: Take your everyday, ordinary life-*
*your sleeping, eating, going-to-work, and walking around life and place it before God as an offering. Embracing what God does for you is the best thing you can do for him.*
*Don't become so well adjusted to your culture that you fit into it without even thinking.*
*Instead, fix your attention on God. You'll be changed from the inside out. Readily recognize what he wants from you, and quickly respond to it. Unlike the culture around you, always dragging you down to its level of immaturity, God brings the best out of you, develops well-formed maturity in you.*
*Romans 12:1*

God changed me from the inside out.

But this line of thinking doesn't fit into today's church most of the time.

Imagine you're standing in line in the grocery store and the register breaks. The attendant calls the manager and when she arrives they begin tearing away at the machine trying to fix it. While you are waiting, you notice an extremely attractive female standing behind you, waiting as well. You strike up a conversation with her and eventually it leads to you inviting her to your church. She smiles. You think it's to cover up some sort of pain, when she responds "I'm a stripper." What do you do?

How about this: You're sitting in Church on Sunday, in 'your' seat, and you observe two noticeably gay men walk into your chapel and sit down. They aren't showing any public displays of affection. They are showing reverence and respect for a house of God, but you know they are gay. When the pastor tells you to greet one another, do you approach them? What do you do?

What did Jesus have to say?

He said to love your neighbor as yourself.

What does that mean? Maybe the effect of that statement means something different for everyone. For me, it's very clear. I know I'm messed up. Next to God I don't compare. Without the blood of Christ, I'm a pretty horrible dude compared to God. However, I have a relationship with Jesus, and I have experienced a joy in my life that is just not possible to experience without him. I know that of all the things in the world that have the potential to make me feel good, there is only one thing that no matter how much I have, won't hurt me.

So here I am with a stripper in the grocery store and a couple of gay guys in church.

What would Jesus say?

"Follow me."

A few months back I was intrigued to find out that there was a ministry concerned with cutters. Not an object used for cutting, but people who cut themselves for relief from their problems. Imagine being so torn up inside, so confused and hurt, that the only way to find comfort is to take a razor and slice your skin. Doesn't sound too therapeutic does it? I have always had a heart for broken youth and I read this story about a ministry designed to interact the some of the most broken of youth. So a couple of followers of Christ are sitting with a young lady who is drunk and high on cocaine in a drug house. This young lady takes the razor she used for cutting her coke, goes to the bathroom and carves "fuck up" on her arm. The followers of Christ tell her Jesus wants to write love on her arms. They share the love of Jesus. They love her. As they wait for her wounds to heal enough for her to enter rehab, they spend the next few days showing her love like she had never experienced before. They provide her with plenty of coffee, cigarettes, food, rock shows and love, and she makes it to an inpatient treatment center. Love. That is what Jesus said.

When are we going to get the point?

When am I going to get the point?

In the book of Mark, the writer tells a story of Jesus' encounter with "madman". Jesus and his disciples get out of their boat after crossing the Sea of Galilee and they are immediately met by a lunatic that lives in the cemetery that constantly cries and cuts himself. He cuts, or slashes, himself. Jesus loves him. Jesus understands that this man is afflicted. Jesus understands that this man needs healing. The man is healed in an unconventional way to say the least, and sent on his way to tell his family of the glory of God.

Jesus loved the hell out of this guy.

I think I get it.

We've had quite enough time to get "it". Jesus spelled it out for us. God showed us more love than we deserve. Stop picking out every one and everything that doesn't agree with what our idea of a Christian is and start loving the hell out of people.

God gave us his only begotten son; I'm unable to give someone the next spot in line. God gave us completely undeserving mercy and grace; I'm unable to keep from cursing when a woman yells at me in a store.

Jesus said to a completely undeserving man, "follow me." He loved me so much he didn't tell me to change everything I am. He didn't say stop doing this, stop doing that. He didn't say anything but "follow me." Jesus knew the change will come when I accept him. He will change me. I won't change anything. He owns the dream. He and only he can change me from the inside out. Jesus loves me no matter how much I screw up. No matter how much I question his authority over the universe even though he has shown me miracle after miracle. Jesus loves each and every one of us.

In the adult Sunday school class I taught I asked a question and got a surprising response.

"Does Jesus love everyone?"

"Is it safe to say that Jesus loves everyone?"

Most said yes, and many said no. Wow. Are we so confused that we as Christians, attending church are unable to understand the most wonderful message in the world?

Can God hate fags?

*"…You shall love your neighbor as yourself."*
*Matthew 22:39*
*NKJV*

Love your neighbor as you love yourself.

I think of people I'm unable to love.

Child molesters.

Does God hate them?

Certainly not.

"For God so loved the World he gave his only begotten son"

That was Jesus talking to a religious leader named Nicodemus. What he didn't say was God so loved parts of the world that he gave his only begotten son. He didn't say God so loved the world that he gave his only begotten son for a few of the deserving people he likes.

Jesus was not on the cross for some of our sins.

He hung, pierced on the cross, for all of our sins.

For all sinners to have the opportunity to have a relationship with God.

Even those we hate.

He did it for you and me.

He did it for people who do drugs. He did it for those who sleep around. He did it for porn stars and strippers. He did it for cops who get in their 'licks'. He did it for liars and thieves. He did it for young girls who cut and burn themselves.

He said follow me.

Sometimes I forget. Sometimes I still have trouble understanding.

He said "take up your cross and follow me."

Bring your baggage, and c'mon. Let's walk together.

All our junk. All the crap we carry around. Give it up. We have a burden and he will take it from us. Not you.

*"Anyone who intends to come with me has to let me lead. You're not in the driver's seat; I am. Don't run from suffering; embrace it. Follow me and I'll show you how. Self-help is no help at all. Self-sacrifice is the way, my way, to finding yourself, your true self. What kind of deal is it to get everything you want but lose yourself? What could you ever trade your soul for?*
*Matthew 16:24*
*The Message*

I know how hard it is to submit everything you have and everything you are. For years I was just some white trash kid from northwest Florida who believed that life was crap. I grew up hard. I worked hard. You get what you work for. I felt like there was no escape from the torment I was subject to, and subject myself to, each and every day.

Jesus saves.

Jesus doesn't kill.

Jesus doesn't hate.

Jesus doesn't punish.

Jesus said to love. Why do I keep screwing it up? Have you ever tried the old adage "Jesus loves the sinner and hates the sin?" How in the hell does the "un-saved" know, and why in the hell am I concerned with it. If that's your response imagine you're the one speaking to the young prostitute who just carved something vulgar in her arm with a razor. Do you honestly think she cares about Jesus hating the sin she is drowning in? She just took a razor and carved "fuck-up" into her arm. She undoubtedly doesn't know that we love her. She doesn't know that she doesn't have to be anything we think she should be.

How about the stripper you met who is putting food on the table for her child. Every dollar some bastard tucked into her garter belt goes to support her toddler. She's naked and giving a lap-dance to some drunk stranger and there is a young man at home who calls her "mommy". Think she cares about what you or I think about how she's sinning? Doubt it. Evidently she hasn't experienced an unconditional love that has taught her to find her value through God.

The writer of the Book of Hebrews states that God made a new covenant with his people. Not a covenant in writing, but a covenant written in the lining of our heart.

I have been blessed by God enough to experience pain and torment. I have been blessed by God enough to survive it and experience pain and torment in other's lives. I have been blessed enough to have been given a body, mind, heart, and soul to understand what a relationship with Christ means and that without having experienced all I have, I never would have understood how to change people's lives the way I have, and will.

I still wonder about all of those people I believe I am incapable of loving and wonder if I can just say what Jesus said.

"Follow me."

It has been my experience that people buried in sin, hiding from the glory of God, are unjustly angry at God.

They should be angry at us.

We spend so much time studying the subtle nuances of scripture and still yet, we completely destroy the most important message in the world.

You and I have the chance to become heroes. The problem for us is that it doesn't happen the way we think it should happen. The end result doesn't come to fruition the way we want.

People sometimes never get the chance to see what Christ was really teaching us.

I was watching one of my favorite music videos the other day that I have probably seen hundreds of times. This time, for the first time, it made me wonder how many opportunities I have missed to show someone the love of Christ.

More than fifteen years ago I saw, for the first time, a music video by *Pearl Jam* called "Jeremy". Eddie Vedder, the lead singer of Pearl Jam, told in an interview that the song was about a child name Jeremy who shot himself in the head in front of his English Class in 1991. Now, years later here I am, still affected by the desperation of this little boy named Jeremy who found no help in anyone. I thought about this boy's story. I thought about my story. Even though I was unaware of Jeremy Delle's existence or the incident until Eddie Vedder started singing about it, I felt like I knew Jeremy. I felt like Jeremy knew me. I think I *know* Jeremy. I can't help but wonder what would have happened if someone went to Jeremy that fateful morning and said...

"Follow me."

# Learn

*I've been wondering where* I'm gonna get the money to have this book published.

That's stupid.

About two years ago a wonderful lady called and asked me if my non-profit organization was still in operation.

"Of course", I say.

She proceeds to tell me that she has "run into" a little money and she feels like God wants her to do a little something with some of it.

She then tells me that she wants to buy "a few" bibles and she wants to know if I can get them into the hands of soldiers going to Iraq.

I tell her it won't be a problem and assure her that it won't be difficult to place a few bibles into the hands of a few soldiers. "Just have them sent to my office and I'll take care of the rest".

Two days later, 2,394 bibles end up on the door-step of my office.

Two-thousand, three-hundred, ninety-four.

Hand to forehand in disbelief I say, "How am I going to get rid of twenty-four hundred bibles?"

A few days later, I learn that a division Chaplain didn't have enough money left in his budget to buy bibles to supply the thousands of troops being deployed.

I have the tendency to repeatedly ask God how I am supposed to do something, and every time I do...

God says, "You're not...

*I am.*"

# The Black Spidey Suit

*"Whoever fights monsters should see to it that in the process he does not become a monster. And if you gaze long enough into an abyss, the abyss will gaze back into you.*
*–Friedrich Nietzsche–*

*Here I am as two* very different guys occupying the same body.

One of them is a God fearing, God-loving man, who wishes he could save the world. He wants to do it with God's Word. That guy is honestly attached to showing love to those who need it. He has a true and caring heart and would deny himself to help others. He wants to handle all problems the way Jesus would.

With patience, and love, and self denial.

This guy knows very well that God is in control and those who oppress and violate innocent people will answer to *Him*.

The other guy is, well...an asshole. Same goal as the first guy, but different way to get there. Just beat the shit out of anything that gets in the way of peace and happiness. You wanna hurt someone? Try me, he says.

This guy knows very well that God is in control and those who oppress and violate innocent people need to have their ass kicked.

He's abrasive, he's rough, and he's the guy you want to be when you have to stand up for yourself.

He knows God is in control but wants to use every ability God gave him to lash out at evil with evil.

I'm not the first to recognize an internal struggle within our souls. You see, recognizing it isn't the problem for me.

The problem is the addiction to both.

I want to be the nice guy.

I want to be the mean guy.

I have seen that both are necessary for my life.

I need them.

Nice guy's stress is very low; things seem easier for him.

Mean guy's ability and willingness to fight has proved to be critically necessary at times.

Nice guy wants to lie in the bed and pray that he doesn't get beaten on a beautiful Saturday morning.

Mean guy wants to get up and go ask for the beating and then burn the house down.

I often want to tap into the dark side of who I am. I want to use the dark side of who I am just enough to get the job done.

Sometimes I need it.

As a cop, when someone who has severely beaten his wife refuses to be placed in handcuffs I know who has to do it.

Nice guy who has immense love and trust in people can't because he wants to believe they made a mistake and will never do it again.

Mean guy knows if he doesn't get this dirt-bag in cuffs, something far worse may happen.

Nice guy won't cross-face someone and throw them to the ground without reserve to protect the safety of others.

As a soldier in a combat zone, when an unauthorized van has just breached the last barrier and is headed for the base camp gate at a high rate of speed, I know who has to stop it.

Nice guy wants to explain to Mr. Van that the consequences of his actions are detrimental.

Mean guy knows if Mr. Van makes it to the gate, eight other soldiers may die.

Nice guy doesn't want to use a weapon.

Mean guy stands in the direct path of the van and fires.

There is a fine line between these two, and believe me, nothing on earth can help me walk it.

It has to be turned on and off.

Most of the time, it's automatic.

Timing is everything.

*For if anyone is a hearer of the word and not a doer,*
*he is like a man observing his natural face in a mirror;*
*for he observes himself, goes away,*
*and immediately forgets what kind of man he was.*
*James 1:23-24*
*NKJV*

I took my family to see *Spiderman 3*. Spiderman's suit is permeated by an alien life form which amplifies characteristics of its host. But it's bad. Peter (Spiderman), like everyone else in the world, also has nice guy and mean guy. But Peter Parker hasn't been able to tap into mean guy. So Peter Parker becomes overtaken by this thing which helps Spidey and Peter be mean guy. Peter feels more powerful. Peter has confidence. Peter Parker begins to peer into an abyss of darkness. He now has the choice between the red-suit Spidey or the black-suit Spidey. One particular scene shows Peter Parker open his closet to retrieve his Spidey-suit. Something a little worse than usual is happening and Peter seems to have lost trust in nice guy's ability to get the job done. Stupid red suit. Peter opens a trunk, holds up the black suit, and smiles.

Peter is gazing into the darkness, and the darkness is gazing right back.

Peter chooses the black suit.

Most of the time, I do very well separating the two.

My patience level has grown far beyond my wildest dreams. I thought I would take a break from coaching third and fourth grade boy's basketball this year only to find myself coaching my daughters third and fourth grade girl's team.

With the boys I feel like they are my men! I can tell them to "pay attention" with a stern voice and they reply "yes-sir!" with enthusiasm.

With the girls I get the feeling that they know perfectly well who's in charge and it ain't me. I tell them "pay attention ladies" and one replies in a high pitched voice, "Coach Ben, your nostrils are crooked." I know darling, I know. Trying to teach an eight year old girl to set up a pick or box somebody out takes a level of patience I never thought attainable.

I thought I'd take a break.

Evidently, God had a different plan.

Two days later I'm standing in the middle of a highway at 3 in the morning next to a 20 year-old girl who was ejected from her car. The car is nearly forty feet away from where this young lady is laying. I see a Spiderman toy on the road amidst a trail of the girls belongings. I learn she has a 2 year-old son...who is now an orphan.

The next day a drunk is telling me to screw myself and I have to fight him to the ground.

The next day I'm in a store with my children and a store clerk screams at me.

Dizzying.

Now, at this moment...

I'm confused.

The switch...is it on or off?

Everything is blurry.

I'm not even thinking.

Where is that fine line now?

What "plan" God has for me?

In the Spiderman 3 movie, the more Peter uses the black Spidey suit, the more the black Spidey suit takes over. Every time Peter gazes into the abyss, the abyss gazes right back.

*Come near to God and he will come near to you.*
*Wash your hands, you sinners, and purify your hearts, you double-minded.*
*James 4:8*
*NIV*

God has blessed my wife and I with two beautiful, wonderful children. My children are usually very well behaved, and respectful. When they were toddlers they received the occasional 'pop' on the backside which probably didn't hurt their diaper covered behind nearly as much as their feelings.

Not long ago, my son was having an issue with bringing home the required materials he needed to complete homework assignments. After restrictions from television, movies, video games and even toys at one point, I told him the next step was a spanking. I explained to him that he was going to end up getting a spanking with a belt. For a short time, the problem was resolved. Then one day he forgot to bring home the most important school project of the year, which was due the next day.

I asked him if he knew what the consequence was going to be and he told me that he did as tears began to well up in his eyes. I told him to go to his room and wait.

For the next few minutes, my wife watched me as I nervously paced around our bedroom with a belt in my hand. I kept saying, "I don't have a choice. I have to do it."

I went into his room, and shut the door behind me.

I asked him if he thought he deserved a spanking and he replied, "yes-sir", in tears.

I was so nervous I stood there with him in silence for almost five minutes.

He's bawling.

I decided to go ahead and get it over with.

I took him gently by the shoulder, turned him around, raised the belt and...

at that moment,

I thought of Fernand.

I stood there holding the belt in the air for a few moments and knew,
I wasn't going to do it.

I knew I had not the ability to do it.

I gave him a light squeeze on the shoulder, lowered the belt, and
walked out of his room.

Unable to look my wife in the eye, I told her with a choked up voice,
"I can't do it."

I leashed my dog, and went for a walk.

Sometimes, we all want to wear the black spidey suit.

# Inappropriate

*What do you say to* a woman who has taken every bottle of pain-killers she owns in an attempt to kill herself?

What do you say to her when you learn she only has a few months to live due to being terminally ill with cancer, and her husband just left her because he didn't want to deal with her sickness or death?

Still seems a little inappropriate to talk about Jesus doesn't it?

Actually, I can't think of a better time to do it.

In the book of John, the disciples and Jesus come across a man who has been blind from birth. The disciples ask Jesus whose sin caused this guy's physical disability; his parents or him? Jesus tells them they are asking the wrong question. The question is not "who sinned?" but "how can God be glorified?".

I have a friend who's gay.

I've only known him for a couple of days, but I still feel like he's my friend.

He has AIDS and he's dying.

He has never known what it's like to have a relationship with Christ.

He only knows what he hears from Christians all the time.

"God hates fags."

"Homosexuals are going to hell."

I wonder, "what if my friend heard what Jesus really said?"

"…Love one another as I have loved you."
John 15:12

My friend has lost his eyesight from the disease and is becoming increasingly more delusional. He hasn't seen a doctor in months and at four in the morning he's talking to people who aren't there. He thinks he's still in his home state, thousands of miles away. He's angry at his mother and stepfather because they won't allow him to watch television. He's telling me how badly his mother treats him and pauses to ask her to get him a coke very politely. She brings him a coke, he tells her thank you and that he loves her. Moments later he's telling me about how badly his mother treats him.

As he is carried away on a stretcher and placed into the back of an ambulance, I watch his mother kiss him on the cheek.

"I love you baby." She tells him as she kisses him again.

"I love you too, mom."

I realize "GOD is right here, right now" and I'm consumed in the moment. The world makes perfect sense. My heart at that moment is so in love with Christ it hurts. My heart is aching at the beauty of this scene and God has allowed me to witness it.

My friend is on his death bed.

I will visit him in the hospital and tell him I love him…

because it's true.

I will tell him Jesus loves him…

because it's true.

I find it very inappropriate to not share the Love of Jesus.

I find it very inappropriate to assume he's on his way to hell.

*About this time Jesus was informed that Pilate had murdered some people from Galilee as they were offering sacrifices at the Temple. "Do you think those Galileans were worse sinners than all the other people from Galilee?" Jesus asked. "Is that why they suffered? Not at all! And you will perish, too, unless you repent of your sins and turn to God. And what about the eighteen people who died when the tower in Siloam fell on them? Were they the worst sinners in Jerusalem? No, and I tell you again that unless you repent, you will perish, too."*
*Luke 13:1-5*
*NLT*

After every terrorist attack, hurricane, flood, or earthquake, genocidal slaughter or disease epidemic, someone decides to let everyone know how horribly the victims were acting leading up to the tragedy. This someone likes to illustrate how sinful the victims were. But that's not what example Jesus left for us to learn from.

Is my friend gonna go to hell?

Hell no.

# Because God

*For he is God's minister to you for good.*
*But if you do evil, be afraid;*
*for he does not bear the sword in vain;*
*for he is God's minister,*
*an avenger to execute wrath on him who practices evil.*
*Romans 13:4*
*NKJV*

*I was on patrol as* a Deputy Sheriff less than four hours before I chased down, and arrested a man.

Now, I was bringing it back to the bad guy.

This time, I knew why I was bringing it back to the bad guy. I am still bringing it back to the bad guy. There comes a point when you're chasing another human being that you realize; you are in fact chasing another human being.

A convenience store clerk just got choked and robbed by the guy I'm chasing after. I'm dodging cars and trying desperately not to get run over while not allowing him to put much more distance between us. After a short distance, he knows I'm going to catch him, so he stops and surrenders.

I started listening to what God is saying to me.

I pray before I go to work at night. I try and remember that I am working for HIM. I ask him to use me as an instrument of HIS work. I ask HIM to speak to me, and most importantly, I ask him to help me hear him when he does.

A mother is home alone late at night with her infant child and sees a man staring at her through the front-door window. Before I get there, the lady sees the man hiding in the shadows trying to open her windows to the room in which she is hiding. As I exit my patrol car I hear him sneaking away though a vacant wooded property. After a quick run, he unsuccessfully tries to hide on his own front porch a couple of blocks away.

As I strap on my bullet proof vest while getting ready for work, I ask God to keep me safe. I ask HIM to keep safe all of us on duty.

A mother wakes up a week before Christmas to find her 8 week old baby isn't breathing. As I watch the father pick the child up and kiss her I want to quit this job. The medical examiner tells the parents it's time to take the baby away and the father volunteers to carry her out to the examiner's van. When he kisses her again as he places her inside the van the breath is knocked out of me.

It's GOD's work. I remind myself every night I go to work. It's not about me, it's about God. What I do every night I work is worship HIM.

I thank him for allowing me to experience all I have experienced. It has made me who I am. It has given me an education I otherwise would never have received.

I make mistakes. I say things I shouldn't. I get dangerously complacent. Most of the time, the job can be boring. I start believing every call I'm dispatched to is a bunch of bull. Everyone's a liar, even when they're telling the truth. Nothing is what it seems.

A friend of mine told a lady once; "you want me to immediately restore order to a situation it took you 18 years to screw up."

When I start getting confused, God makes me aware. I start remembering why I'm doing, what I'm doing.

When I'm getting ready for work, I put a loaded magazine into my pistol, and charge a round into the chamber. I sometimes remember a Psalm of David, and I pray…

*Blessed be the Lord my rock,*
*who trains my hands for war,*
*and my fingers for battle–…*
*Psalm 144:1*
*NKJV*

I was headed to a call and had no idea where it was. It was a "domestic" call in which a female called 911 and reported that her husband was drunk, screaming, and smashing out the windows of the house.

"Great." I thought.

 "I already have three reports to do."

The thought of having to do another report is bothering me. I'm not concerned with the fact that it is a domestic call, or that this drunk guy is smashing out the windows in the house, or that he may have or may be doing something horrible to whomever is calling in.

The dispatcher gives me an update while I'm still headed there. She tells me that Mr. Drunk is running around outside and the wife and children are locked inside the house.

I had no problem whatsoever finding the house. Our county's address system is setup in a way in which one can find just about anything just by knowing the address. However, sometimes problems arise because roads dead-end and continue elsewhere. Had I not been in the right place at the right time, I would not have taken the only road that led to the house. There was one way in, and one way out.

As I pulled up into nearly complete darkness, I saw the shadow of a man crouching down in a sort of attack position holding something in each hand.

"This is different." I thought.

Most domestic calls usually end up with one of the parties immediately coming out to your patrol vehicle to tell you what a wonderful person they are and what a horrible person they're married to.

This guy is ducking in and out of the shadow of a beat-up pick-up truck holding some undistinguishable objects in his hands.

I got out of the car trying never to take my eyes off of the silhouette. I could tell he was taller than me. Maybe six-feet, four-inches.

"Deputy Adams with the Sheriff's Office, let me see your hands." I announce as I enter the yard and stop about forty feet away from him.

"You wanna see my hands?" he screamed. "Then fucking shoot me!"

After only a moment, my .45 cleared leather.

He leapt from the shadows holding a four-way lug wrench in one hand, and a 1½ foot long 'breaker-bar in the other screaming "shoot me!" as he ran toward me.

Deadly force: Authorization to kill or cause great bodily harm or injury.

This is where things get interesting in the lives of a cop.

We have the next few infinitesimal moments to make a decision that is going to change to course of lives forever.

I can shoot this person right smack dab in the center of his chest and end his life…to protect myself and, incidentally, at his request.

Or I can decide to retreat.

I have often heard not to take your work home with you at the end of the day. I have also heard not to take your home life to work with you.

This day, or night as it was, which spidey suit was I wearing? Was this situation extreme enough to reset any preset conditions or personality grievances I was dealing with?

It disturbs me to think of the inestimable number of factors that had to be perfectly set into place for that situation to have come together exactly as it had. Each moment in the lives of these two men has fatefully crossed their paths with each man standing on vastly different shores of good and evil.

I am standing in darkness, illuminated slightly by a laser emitted from the grip of my .45 caliber pistol, facing an inevitable attack and I am standing on vastly different shores of courage and cowardice within myself.

I didn't retreat.

I took a step back to steady myself and stopped.

He reached a distance of twenty feet away, and I put pressure on the trigger.

He stopped and I could see he was crying. He was breathing heavily, bouncing, and rocking back and forth, and every muscle in his body was flexed from his tension and his anger.

I keyed up my radio and let the dispatcher know it would be a good time to send a back-up unit…quickly.

"Throw your weapons down and show me your hands, now!

"Fuck you, just shoot me…just fucking shoot me. I can't take this anymore."

He turned around and began to run back to the shadows and I followed, keeping a safe distance. We had only gone a few feet when a lady came running toward me from the darkness around the house crying.

"Oh God please help us sir! Our kids are inside."

Now, I'm not usually one to complain about the stress of a situation but damn. If dealing with a drunk desiring suicide by cop isn't enough, I've got kids in the house to deal with.

I tell the lady to get behind me and get behind my car out by the road.

She tells me his name is Darren and she doesn't know what is wrong with him.

"Has he ever done this before?" I ask.

"No. Never." She's lying I think.

Darren starts running toward me swinging his weapons again and I yell for her to get behind my car.

I take a step forward. I plant my feet and tell him to stop.

At twenty feet I'm putting pressure on the trigger and tell him to stop again.

He stops and screams at me.

"I just want the pain to stop so fucking shoot me!"

He takes another two steps swinging his weapons screaming "Shoot me mother-fucker, shoot me!" and stops.

"Put down your weapons Darren! I don't want to shoot you dammit, put that shit down and show me your hands and knock this shit off!"

He turns to walk away screaming. I keep repeating that I don't want to shoot him and for him to throw down his weapons.

He keeps telling me "if you wanna see my hands so bad just shoot me."

His crying intensified as did his intermittent screaming.

His screams were very deep, growling, devilish screams. No words. Just screams.

"I want to help you Darren, so put that shit down."

"You're not gonna help me." He's talking now…"I just want the pain to stop."

Screaming again, "I need help so just shoot me!"

He paced back and forth, dropped his weapons, and started to walk away from them.

He knew I was coming for them. I quickly began closing the gap between myself and his weapons and after he had taken only a few steps, he turned around and picked them back up. He's about twelve feet away and lunges toward me.

When I went through Marine Corps boot camp I learned a great number of lessons. One of which was 'Hitting Skills'. The main portion of the 'hitting skills' lesson was standing in a 4'X4' ring with your opponent punching the sense out of each other. One bout was three rounds, thirty seconds a piece. There was no ducking or dodging, no bobbing or weaving. Feet firmly planted, rotate at the waist and shoulders, drive with your legs and punch the face of your opponent as if you are focusing on going straight through to the back of his head. There was no where to go. You stand, you punch, and you get punched. You don't back down. You don't put your head down. Even if keeping your head up means you're giving your opponent a better target. You thank each other for giving confidence in your ability to take a punch. You thank each other for having given each other the pride in knowing you have the "cajones" to stand in the face of pain and take it out of sheer will.

But even as ridiculous as this educational experience seems, I knew even then, what the lesson was really about.

Not only was the purpose missed by most outsiders, most Marines passed it over without second glance.

Had the Marine Corps been acutely aware of the purpose of hitting skills, they would not have allowed it to have been discontinued as part of training.

The purpose?

Think.

That's it.

You are repeatedly getting punched in the face. You are getting hit more times than most professional fighters do in an entire fight.

It's a little stressful.

It hurts.

Imagine your brain is trying to process your normal motor functions along with all the pain and overwhelming stress you're going through.

So while you are randomly throwing punches and getting your face re-arranged something interesting happens.

You begin to think.

You can't learn all you need to know about hitting someone in just a few hours of lessons spanning over only a few days.

But you can learn to think.

I received a concussion the first day of hitting skills and I never felt better. I never knew how good it actually felt to hold your head up and ask for more.

If you can learn to think and clear your mind under such intense conditions, your ability to fight is significantly greater. You will be able to make better decisions faster.

It was a gift I never lost.

Think.

"STOP!"

Darren stands eight feet away.

"Darren, put 'em back down dude."

He dropped the tools, stepped forward, and dropped to his knees sobbing.

I tell him to lay down and put his hands behind his back.

He looks at me, and very calmly asks, "You want my hands behind my back?"

"Shoot me!" he screams as he lunges toward me...again.

I holstered my weapon and drew my "taser" and he stopped.

He laid on the ground crying harder than I've ever seen a grown man cry.

My back-up unit arrived moments after Darren finally surrendered.

I holstered my "taser" and placed Darren in hand-cuffs.

After I took a deep breath, I said "Darren, roll over on to your butt and we're gonna stand you up..alright?"

I walked him to the car and he's still crying.

I tell him to sit in my car in the air conditioning and try to cool down.

"I don't give a fuck about air-conditioning I just want help. You said you would help me."

"I'm gonna help you Darren, but I think we need to take a breather."

My investigation revealed that Darren had never been arrested. He had never even had a ticket from what I could see. His wife and teenage children told me that Darren had never hit them. They went even further to say that he has never been violent with anyone. They must be lying, I was thinking. But they weren't. I couldn't find his name in any police report. No one had ever even alleged that Darren had done something criminal.

A few years ago, Darren suffered from severe head trauma. Although he is able to function normally, his wife and children said he hasn't been the same since. Darren's physical pain compounded with stress and little or no treatment had finally climaxed. He wanted the physical and emotional pain to stop. He was hurting so bad he wanted to die, but he knew he couldn't do it himself.

So God sent me.

Two days before this incident happened, I was at a "men's fellowship" with close friends. I told them I was going to write a book and that I had a working title. They asked me what it was and this is how I responded…

"How do you act like a Christian while holding a gun to someone's face?"

Laughter erupted as we were amused by that, and we all joked about it for quite a few minutes afterward.

I didn't realize that God was listening.

I didn't realize God was going to answer my question so soon.

Everyone asks me why I didn't shoot Darren when he charged at me with the lug-wrench and breaker bar. I tell them I didn't want to, and I'm glad I didn't.

If I were to be completely honest when asked, it would take writing a book to answer.

Most of my colleagues tell me they would have shot him. I'm not sure how true that is but it makes me wonder; had anyone else responded to that call, Darren may have been killed.

A few months after the incident, I received a letter from Darren.

A court-ordered apology letter.

Although it was court-ordered, I sensed something better. Darren was asking me for forgiveness… through the love of Christ. Darren explained that God was doing wonderful things in his life and he thanked me for not killing him. Darren said he owes me his life and he and his wife and children pray for my safety.

*And that about wraps it up. God is strong, and he wants you strong. So take everything the Master has set out for you, well-made weapons of*

*the best materials. And put them to use so you will be able to stand up to everything the devil throws your way. This is no afternoon athletic contest that we'll walk away from and forget about in a couple of hours. This is for keeps, a life or death fight to the finish against the devil and all his angels.*
*Ephesians 6:10-12*
*The Message*

# A Moment

*You therefore must endure hardship as a good soldier of Jesus Christ.*
*No one engaged in warfare entangles himself with the affairs of this life,*
*that he may please him who enlisted him as a soldier.*
*2 Timothy 2:3–4*
*NKJV*

*It's been a hell of* a ride.

Since I have been writing about my life I can't help but think of how this life has been so full of adventures, good and bad. Even though it's been a little rough, I love every bit of it. Every struggle, every proverbial mountain I have had to climb, every pit I have fallen into, I smile when I sometimes think of them all together.

I was listening to "Somewhere Over the Rainbow/What a Wonderful World", sung by Hawaiian man named Israel while I was cooking dinner for my family. I slung my hand towel over my shoulder and I thought of how blessed I am to have experienced such a life. As I stared into the boiling water, the music played, and my life seemed to play in my head like a movie montage.

There were scenes of great laughter and happiness mixed with moments of great sadness. Visions of setting up the Christmas tree or laying on the floor with my father listening to Ben E. King, holding my brother's hand as his life slowly faded away, losing a high school sweetheart, breaking down in the middle of the road with my mother without 95 cents for a gallon of gas, and running from communist armies with my friends.

*Well I see trees of green and red roses too*
*I'll watch them bloom for me and you*
*And I think to myself*
*What a wonderful world*

The wife and kids and I were having a disco dancing moment after dinner tonight. I realized how ridiculous we all were and I fell in love with the moment. I think at that moment, I realized how much in love with my wife and my children I really am.

I then realized how much in love God is with me.

I think often of the past. Only to learn.

I have no regrets, and I wouldn't change a thing.

Not one moment.

I think of the future and know I have a long journey still ahead, and I know God has a lot planned for me.

I can't wait.

Lamentations 3:51
The Message

Romans 12:3
The Message

Luke 12:49
NLT

Ecclesiastes 4:1-3
The Message

Psalm 72:14
NKJV

James 1:2-4
The Message

James 1:23-24
NKJV

James 4:8
NIV

Ephesians 2:1-6
The Message

1 Corinthians 7:17
The Message

Psalm 18:17-18
NKJV

2 Corinthians 7:10
The Message

Ephesians 4:17
The Message

Lamentations 3:18
The Message

Lamentations 3:16-18
The Message

Genesis 2:16-17
The Message

Genesis 3:2-5
The Message

Ecclesiastes 2:9-11
The Message

John 11:35
KJV

2 Timothy 1:3-4
The Message

Romans 1:28
The Message

Luke 12:48
NKJV

Ephesians 1:11
The Message

Jeremiah 1:5
NKJV

Ecclesiastes 8:2-7
The Message

John 21:19
NKJV

John 21:15
NIV

John 21:16
NIV

Mark 16:15
The message

Matthew 22:37
NKJV

Luke 6:27
NKJV

Luke 10:27
NKJV

John 3:16
NKJV

John 13:34
NKJV

John 15:12
NKJV

John 15:17
NIV

John 14:27
NKJV

John 16:33
NKJV

Romans 12:1
The Message

Matthew 22:39
NKJV

Matthew 16:24
The Message

Romans 12:1-2
The Message

John 9:1-2
The Message

John 15:12
NKJV

Luke 13:1-5
NLT

Romans 13:4
NKJV

Psalm 144:1
NKJV

Ephesians 6:10-12
The Message

2 Timothy 2:3-4
NKJV

# Special Thanks…

*God. For everything. For this* body, this mind, this heart and this soul. Especially for your son. Please don't stop talking to me and more importantly, allow me to hear you when you do. Please don't ever stop allowing me to work for you. I am in love with all you are.

Lavonne, thank you for listening to my incessant rambling and making this journey with me. I'm more in love with you now than ever. Ben & Gladys, for being so wonderful for allowing me to make every answer to your questions more complicated than they need to be. You two are freakin' awesome. Mom, for teaching me how to hang in there, never give up, and for just being an overall great mom. Dad, teaching me to give until you've got nothing left, to toughen up at just the right times and shaping an image of God. Amanda, for getting lost with me. Brandon, allowing me to stick with you. Jason, I love you and I miss you dearly. We've got a lot to catch up on. Grandma, making me feel important. Grandpa, for showing me how a hero behaves. Bigdaddy, for teaching me to take as long as I damn well please to tell a story. Mamaw, for much needed "anything I want" time. Jim, Beth and Nic, for making me a part of your family at a critical time in my life. Doug for taking care of my mother. Sandie for taking care of my father and for just being you. Amanda, Miranda and Tom, for believing in family. I love all of you more than you can possibly imagine. Fernand and Burt, I hope you started a conversation with *HIM*.

Ramos, Brooks, Brewster for being the most loyal and dedicated friends a guy could have before, during and beyond the war. And no, we'll not be paying anyone a visit. Andrew, Jonathan, Dave, Lawren for experiencing God like no one I've ever seen before you. Our conversations will never end; exactly as it should be. Marie just for allowing me to be your friend. Sarah for correcting me. Dr Phillip Haines for baptizing me and starting this whole conversation ten years later. Dr Ed Johnson, I wrote this whole thing from your chair. Dr Mark Cummins for packing lunch.

Ed and Kurt for giving me a chance and showing me how Godly statesman should act. Zack, Bobby, Lisa, Paul, Darius, Steve, Sting, Scott, Mike; for being my perpetual FTO's.

# Soundtrack

*O.M.D-Dreaming, Michael Jackson-Beat it, Concrete* Blonde-Jenny I read, Five Finger Death Punch-The Bleeding, Shinedown-.45/Burning Bright/I Dare You, Dolly Parton-Smokey Mountain Memories, Mel Street-Smokey Mountain Memories, Bob Dylan-Knockin' on Heaven's Door, Johnny Cash-Peace in the Valley, Disturbed-Land of Confusion, Survivor-Eye of the Tiger, Journey-Don't Stop Believing, Israel KamakawiwoʻOle-Somewhere Over the Rainbow, Breaking Benjamin-Until the End/Breathe, When In Rome-The Promise, Social Distortion-Ball and Chain/Wrong, Skid Row-18 and Life/I remember you/Quicksand Jesus/Together We Stand, Linkin Park-What I've Done/Hands Held High/Crawling, Pearl Jam-Jeremy, Pixies-Where is my Mind?/Debaser

43244177R00093